1 MONTH OF
FREE
READING

at

www.ForgottenBooks.com

By purchasing this book you are eligible for one month membership to ForgottenBooks.com, giving you unlimited access to our entire collection of over 1,000,000 titles via our web site and mobile apps.

To claim your free month visit:

www.forgottenbooks.com/free262764

ISBN 978-0-483-76376-0
PIBN 10262764

This book is a reproduction of an important historical work. Forgotten Books uses state-of-the-art technology to digitally reconstruct the work, preserving the original format whilst repairing imperfections present in the aged copy. In rare cases, an imperfection in the original, such as a blemish or missing page, may be replicated in our edition. We do, however, repair the vast majority of imperfections successfully; any imperfections that remain are intentionally left to preserve the state of such historical works.

JUDICIAL MURDER

The Case of Lieutenant Wark

BY

E. R. GRAIN, LL.D.

JUDICIAL SCANDALS AND ERRORS

II.

WATFORD, LONDON

THE UNIVERSITY PRESS, LIMITED

1900

THE UNIVERSITY PRESS

JUDICIAL MURDER.

THE CASE OF LIEUTENANT WARK.

THE land of Judge Jeffreys in matters judicial is in a peculiar position; the masses and the uninitiated are convinced that our law, if not the acme of perfection, is very near to this desirable condition, and that the administration of the law is in the best hands; that any improvements which might be required, in altering an antiquated system, are in due course effected by our legislators. Lawyers know better, but they have every reason to be silent, and the honest counsel agrees with Mephistopheles:—

> "I know what science this has come to be.
> All rights and laws are still transmitted
> Like an eternal sickness of the race,—
> From generation unto generation fitted,
> And shifted round from place to place.
> Reason becomes a sham, Beneficence a worry:
> Thou art a grandchild, therefore woe to thee!
> The right born with us, ours in verity,
> This to consider, there's, alas! no hurry."

We English are worse off in this respect than other nations because the hypocritical spirit permeating and poisoning every branch of life has also entered here. We continue to admire where contempt, or at least inquiry, should take the place of admiration. We have to contend with a rotten system and with the ingrained cant and hypocrisy of which judges less than other mortals have freed themselves.

The honesty of English judges consists mainly in their incorruptibility, their inaccessibility to bribes. The (in other civilised countries unheard of) power vested in a single judge, the imbecility of a common jury, and the prejudice of the justices constitute a real danger, and miscarriages of justice are more frequent in this country than in France or Germany. And the worst feature is that such miscarriages, whether brought about by malice and per-

(1)

jury or by judicial errors, are irreparable, as far as the criminal procedure is concerned. The power vested in the Home Secretary is sheer mockery, and we may take it as an indisputable fact that errors committed by judge and jury, no matter for what cause, are irreparable.

With astonishment mingled with contempt we have looked upon the case of Captain Dreyfus, and we have proudly asserted "that such things cannot happen in England."

I would rather affirm that worse cases happen in dear old England, and I see in the revision of the Dreyfus case a healthy sign, and a useful experience besides.

In England a convict has no means whatever to have his case re-opened, no attempt to rehabilitate an innocently condemned man has the remotest possibility of success. No Court of Criminal Appeal is in existence and no Court of Cassation. Judicial murder is absolutely final. And judicial scandals abound in consequence. But they are hushed up by mutual consent of the press, and even the worst cases are ignored. That is the reason, the sole reason, why we have no Dreyfus cases in England.

The public is ignorant of the intricacies of the law and of the law procedure, lawyers, and all those who are in the know, are silent, and so we are at a standstill, which is as dangerous as retrogression.

Open outrages like those committed by Judge Jeffreys are less pernicious than the system which sends innocent men to penal servitude and perdition.

A judicial system, bad at its root, but considered sound by the masses, approved by the people, is a national danger of the gravest sort, but the attempt to improve or to mend is hopeless as long as no voice is raised from those who know, or who ought to know, what is going on behind the scenes.

The advantages of the jury system, healthy in itself, are frustrated by the absurd power vested in a single judge, and by the constitution of the jury. The judge with the greatest ease transmits his prejudice to the jury, and in most cases makes use, honestly in his way, of his influence. Some ridiculous cases, showing this, happen now and then. A jury at the Old Bailey, misunderstanding the direction of the judge, returns a verdict of "not guilty." The judge is indignant, and the willing jury returns with new directions to find the prisoner "guilty" according to his advice.

If amongst a servile jury one or two independent men should differ from the judge's opinion and advice, a very simple method remains open to the prosecution to obtain a conviction. The case is brought before another jury and before the same biassed judge until a conviction is obtained. This experiment can be repeated indefinitely and is always successful. It seems a kind of ambition of the judge to finally find a jury who is entirely of his opinion, and there is no difficulty in doing so.

I was present at the Old Bailey some years ago when in a libel case the Recorder in his summing-up showed the greatest bias against the accused, but the jury disagreed. Prosecutor's counsel, seeing his chance in the Recorder's prejudice against the accused, at once proposed to try the case with another jury. Counsel for the defence protested against the Recorder hearing the case again, and proposed that it should go before another judge. In vain, the Recorder decided to try the case again with another jury, and this time, bent upon having his view of the libel adopted by the new jury, summed-up with the greatest vigour against the accused with the desired result. This practice is simply scandalous, yet of everyday occurrence and perfectly legal. The sources of error and blunder are more frequent in England than elsewhere, for manifold reasons, which I will touch in another article dealing with this particular subject, and this should be an additional reason to provide for means to repair a great wrong.

The reason why in England comparatively few erroneous convictions come to light, is, as Mr. Th. Stanley and the late J. F. Stephen* rightly pointed out, that we have no efficient machinery for bringing them to light.

The prisoner, taken by surprise by false evidence at the trial, is convicted without having any opportunity of rebutting such evidence, he is hurried off to prison and deprived of the possibility of getting inquiries made into those false statements. His friends and relatives cannot even communicate with the inno-

---

* J. F. Stephen, The History of the Criminal Law, v. Thos. Stanley, Miscarriages of Justice, *Free Review*, Vol. VI., p. 264.

cently convicted, and, besides the farcical application to the Home Secretary, there exist no means whatever to right a grievous wrong.

A man convicted like Captain Dreyfus in this country would, without the possibility of a redress, have remained in prison, and a Dreyfus Scandal would have been an impossibility in England, not because the wrongful conviction was impossible, but because his friends would have had no means to obtain a revision of the wrongful conviction, and because English newspapers under no circumstances whatever take the part of a convict, or insert the appeal of his friends. With a conviction a criminal case is closed for the English press, and there lies the reason why we never hear of Dreyfus cases. Justice Stephen, in this respect, pointedly says *(loc. cit.)* : —

"No provision whatever is made for questioning the decision of a jury on matters of fact. However unsatisfactory a verdict may be—whatever facts may be discovered after the trial, which, if known at the trial, would have altered the result—no means are at present provided by law by which a verdict can be reversed. All that can be done in such a case is to apply to the Queen through the Secretary of State for the Home Department for a pardon for the person wrongly convicted.

"This is one of the greatest defects in our criminal procedure. To pardon a man on the ground of his innocence is itself, to say the least, an exceedingly clumsy mode of procedure; but not to insist upon this it cannot be denied that the system places everyone concerned, and especially the Home Secretary and the judge who tried the case (and who in practice is always consulted), in a position at once painful and radically wrong, because they are called upon to exercise what are really the highest judicial functions without any of the conditions essential to the due discharge of these functions. They cannot take evidence; they cannot hear arguments; they act in the dark, and cannot explain the reasons of the decision at which they arrive."

"The evil is notorious," Justice Stephen concludes, "but it is difficult to find a satisfactory remedy."

In all the continental countries this remedy has been found in a Court of Appeal or of Cassation, and in most civilised States a case can be retried even after the accused has undergone his punishment, if new facts can be brought forward.

In England, where the verdict is absolutely final, and where the whole conduct of a case is placed into the hands of one man, the duty of impartiality becomes more imperative than in countries where at least three and generally five judges divide the responsibility. But English judges at the Old Bailey or at the Assize seem unconscious of this tremendous responsibility. They are all honest and sincere according to their own light, but there is seldom a judge to be found who would abstain from abusing his power, in summing-up, of winning over the jury to his own view of the case, which very often is that of unmitigated prejudice. In common cases of theft, larceny, murder this prejudice naturally is not so evident, as in imaginary crimes, such as blasphemy, libel, and offences against so-called morals.

We know that in actions under the blasphemy laws, which happily are now a thing of the past, the religious conviction of the judge was the only question of importance in the decision of the jury, and the reason why blasphemy proceedings have been abandoned lately is that these religious convictions of judges have been shaken, and the prosecutor, not being able to bring the case before a judge of his own choice, runs the risk of a fiasco and ignominious defeat. Even the jury, composed as it may be of Unitarians, Nonconformists, and Atheists, is not quite reliable, and on the bench Agnostics like Lord Coleridge and Sir J. F. Stephen are not an exception.

Thus Atheism is no longer a crime, but offences against the sixth commandment, which neither in this country nor in any other are punishable by law, are converted into crimes and punished as such with an unheard-of severity. And here the prejudice or partiality of the presiding judge is more dangerous than in any other cases because he can play on the hypocritical side of the jury, which in social life plays such an important part in this country.

We all know that of all nations in the world the English is the most immoral, and appears as the most moral. There is no more debauchery in any city of Europe than in London, no more adultery in any country than in Great Britain, in one day more perjury is committed in the law courts than in the whole of France in a year, and yet we wish to appear as the most moral people on the globe. To maintain this sham, hypocrisy is a *sine qua non*, and the keeping up of appearances is essential. And the, perhaps unconscious, feeling that it is necessary to appear a model of morality while indulging secretly in all sorts of vices, has taken hold of the middle classes, from which the jury is recruited, to such an extent that it is very easy for judge or counsel to utilise that tendency wherever it should seem advisable to do so.

A striking instance is the case of Lieutenant Wark which startled the world, but was hushed up by the action of the Home Secretary, who recommended the commuting of the death sentence into one of three years' penal servitude before public indignation could be aroused against the verdict and sentence.

The crying injustice of the whole affair cannot more clearly be demonstrated than by this action of the Home Secretary, and the three years' penal servitude is a tribute to that hypocritical spirit which prompted the sentence of death on an honourable officer whose only crime was that he had loved too much, and had confided his thoughts and desires, which wiser men bury ·in their hearts, to paper. I have taken the trouble to obtain the verbatim report of this remarkable trial, which will be published in a separate volume, and I will try to give here a summary of the proceedings, which will justify the remarks that I have made.

Robert John Wark, Lieutenant of Royal Engineers, Woolwich, convicted of the murder of Jane Yates, and sentenced to death by Justice Phillimore, immediately afterwards reprieved by the Home Secretary, is, without the least doubt, the victim of English hypocrisy, and as innocent of the crime imputed to him as ever a man was, but guilty of the great crime "immorality," he has been sacrificed on the altar of cant. This Moloch claims his victims year by year, and he must be satisfied.

Lieutenant Wark was a model officer, honest and straightforward, brave and courageous, so that even his enemies at the trial could not shake his reputation as a soldier or man.

The prisoner enlisted as gunner in the Royal Artillery in 1869, was promoted to be bombardier in 1872, made corporal in November 1872, sergeant in 1874, battery sergeant-major in 1878, and regimental sergeant-major in 1883 with the rank as warrant officer. He received his commission as lieutenant on the 10th of August, 1889, after twenty years' service. He served in India for a period of fourteen years—from 1875 to 1889, and went through the Afghan War. He was at Candahar and received the Afghan medal. On obtaining his commission he was appointed adjutant to the second brigade of the artillery volunteers at Liverpool, where he remained for five years and ten months. Then he rejoined his regiment.

Witnesses testified to the fact that Lieutenant Wark was thought very highly of in his regiment, but all this did not avail to dispel the prejudice created by certain voluptuous love letters which the accused in the course of five years had written to his beloved. In the absence of any positive proof of his guilt this prejudice, fostered by the judge, served to convict the accused, simply because it was assumed that a man who would write lascivious letters would also be capable of committing a felony.

From the following observations my readers will see that from the beginning it was evident that Lieutenant Wark was not guilty of the crime of which he was accused, and the medical witnesses should have convinced the jury that the case against this officer was at least extremely doubtful.

Mr. Justice Phillimore, in charging the grand jury, must already have felt that without a special recommendation from his lordship to find a true bill the jury may have thrown out the case. In the course of his *resumé* he said :—

"Gentlemen, there is much that is obscure in this case, much that is difficult, but the main outlines are pretty clear. The man and the woman, and the man being a married man and the woman an unmarried woman about thirty years of age, had undoubtedly lived for several years in immoral relations. The letters from the man to the woman found in the deceased woman's room and possession, disgusting and disgraceful as they are, show an intercourse of a peculiar degree of immorality and lasciviousness which for a long time had taken place between the two. The result was, and of that there can be no doubt, that the woman was pregnant, and that the man knew she was pregnant, and it would rather appear that on some previous occasion, the same thing had happened, and the woman then had procured miscarriage. The letters on the present occasion seem to point to the suggestion of abortion, coming from the deceased woman in the first instance, and it is fair to the prisoner to say that he seems, in the first instance, to have deprecated any such course, and to have advised her to brave the matter out. At the same time there is no doubt, that, being some months gone in pregnancy, abortion was procured, and the result of it was that blood poisoning set in, and within a week or a few days after the probable date of the operation the woman died of blood poisoning. It is for that that this man is put on his trial. I think the woman died about the 26th or 27th of July, and the prosecution seems to point to a particular date—the 20th of July—when the two parties met at Crewe, as the probable date the operation was performed. The man is an officer at Woolwich and the woman lived with her mother at Liverpool. They were apparently accustomed to meet at railway hotels and other places for the purpose of their lust. On this occasion they seem to have met at Crewe, and I think the prosecution suggest that on the 20th of July the operation which led to the abortion was performed at an hotel in Crewe. As I understand it the prosecution lay the charge in either of two ways. They say in the first place that the man actually drove the instrument which effected the miscarriage and resulted in the woman's death; and as he did that with his own hand he committed a felony upon the body of the woman, and, as the result of that felony was the woman's death, he must by law be considered guilty of murder. . . . [Here follows the definition of murder.] . . . The prosecution, I understand, put the case also in another way. They say, it may be that the woman herself—although the doctors think it very improbable that the woman administered the instrument to herself, but if the man stood by, encouraged her, met her for the purpose, procured a room for the purpose, and was by her when she did it, then, in law he is a party to her committing that felonious act. It is as if he had committed it himself, and, as it ended in death, then he is guilty of murder. Well, gentlemen, if you find either of these *prima facie* cases made out to your satisfaction, if there is in your opinion *prima facie* evidence that he was himself the doer of the act, or that he was at any rate a participator, abettor, or assister, it will be your duty to find a true bill, and I imagine, having carefully read the depositions, that you will, without going very minutely into the matter, think it is certainly a case for you to find a true bill and send the man for trial."

Here we have the case in a nutshell: the prisoner has written indecent letters to the deceased, he has met her at hotels, there has been abortion, but how it has been brought about even the prosecution cannot tell, but as the accused, a married man, has written these immoral letters, and as he had met the woman at hotels, the grand jury must find a true bill, a *prima facie* case having been made out by the prosecution. And, of course, the grand jury did find the true bill. The drama commences.

Mr. Pickford, in stating the case for the crown, acknowledged that there was no direct evidence, and that the case rested on the letters written (before the alleged murder) by the accused.

Of the grave doubt expressed by the medical experts whether an operation had taken place at all and whether the miscarriage was a natural one prosecuting counsel did not say a word, but he laid great stress on the indecency of the letters in the same way as the judge had done in his address to the grand jury.

"They were filthy, disgusting letters which one would not have thought it possible for anyone in the position of the prisoner to have written. *The prisoner was a married man and the father of a family.*"

Extracts from Lieutenant Wark's letters, which in themselves could prove nothing beyond that the accused was ever ready to do anything that the deceased wanted him do, could not fail to increase the prejudice against the prisoner, who in one of these letters said : —

"As I have had the greatest pleasure and happiness with you men ever had, I am quite ready to make any sacrifice you may deem expedient."

All the letters produced were in the same strain, and on these the prosecution had based their case. They tried to prove that it was the intention or wish of the deceased that an operation should be performed, and that the prisoner concurred in this intention. The idea that, even supposing that these letters should have the meaning given to them by the prosecuting counsel, there was the necessity to prove that an operation had actually been performed; and, secondly, that the accused's intention had ripened into the deed, did not seem to occupy the prosecuting counsel to a considerable degree.

In one of the letters read by Mr. Pickford Lieutenant Wark clearly advises his beloved to abandon her plan. He writes: "I do hope you will decide on letting things take their course and face it out."

This should impress even the prejudiced with the necessity of proving beyond the least doubt that an operation had taken place, and that the abortion was not a natural one, or one produced by the deceased without the knowledge of Lieutenant Wark.

How utterly the prosecution failed to establish this we shall see if we consider with an impartial spirit the evidence of the medical men who attended the unfortunate lady and made the post-mortem examination.

The prisoner pleaded "not guilty." The first witness for the crown was Mrs. Jane Yates, the mother of the deceased, who asserted that she knew nothing about the whole affair except that her daughter left home on July 20th and returned the following night at 8 o'clock, and that Dr. Shaw informed her of the serious illness of Jane when she was under his care at 120 Salisbury Road. She found Lieutenant Wark's letters, which led to the charge of murder, in her daughter's bedroom.

A stationer proved the receipt of a number of letters on behalf of Miss Yates, and a post-office official testified to the letters having passed through the post office.

Then Samuel Walter Burleigh, the manager of the Railway Hotel at Crewe, said that the prisoner, calling himself Captain Yates, stayed with the deceased lady at the hotel on the 8th and 9th of June, also on the 18th, 19th, and 20th of the same month. The prisoner's letters to Miss Yates were then read to the jury in a voice audible only to the jury as they were considered to be too scandalously indecent for the auditorium.

A chambermaid and a waitress at the Crewe Hotel, where it was alleged the operation took place, could only testify to the presence of Lieutenant Wark and Miss Yates at the hotel on the 20th of July. They said that Miss Yates said to the prisoner: "I feel better, only tired." From this remark in connection with the prisoner's letters the prosecution concluded that an operation had taken place at Crewe, and practically no other evidence pointing to this supposition was adduced.

Another witness, Miss Eleanor Jackson, in whose house Miss Yates died, said that the deceased wrote a letter in pencil addressed to Captain R. Peacock, which runs as follows:—

"My darling Hubby,—I am deadly ill. Shaw has been three times with me to-day. Darling, you do not know what I have suffered. Do come down on Saturday and stay the night. I cannot add more.

"Your sick wifey,

"JEANNIE."

The same witness said that she found in a bag a card-board box with a fœtus. Thus the fact that a miscarriage had taken place was clearly proved, and confirmed by the doctors afterwards.

Miss Yates died of septic peritonitis and pleuritis, commonly called blood-poisoning, and as to this fact all the doctors agreed.

Dr. Frank Thomas Paul, honorary surgeon of the Liverpool Royal Infirmary, made the post-mortem examination, and ascertained the inflammation, and found an insignificant abrasion in the neck of the womb, which in his opinion could have been caused by a catheter or in any other way. It was a very slight abrasion. Counsel asked this expert: "From appearances alone can you say positively whether it was a natural miscarriage or one produced by instruments?" And his answer was as follows:—

"There was nothing in the appearance of the parts which would justify me stating whether it was a natural miscarriage or one produced by instruments. In many cases of the kind it is impossible to say whether an instrument has been used or not. Where the womb is not injured you cannot tell, but in other cases you can speak positively. This is a case in which I could not speak positively."

Mr. Gill cross-examined Dr. Paul, and ascertained that there are a variety of causes which predispose to miscarriage, and that there are many cases in which women produce miscarriage themselves without any assistance. Mr. Gill also elicited the interesting fact that the proportion of natural miscarriages was recognised by medical men to be one to five according to some authorities and one to ten according to others, that is, at least one miscarriage occurs to every ten pregnancies.

Then counsel asked the medical expert: "Is there the slightest difference in the world between peritonitis in an artificially produced miscarriage and peritonitis in a natural miscarriage?"

And Dr. Paul answered: "No, the peritonitis would be the same. If septic peritonitis followed it would be fatal in both cases."

In a similar way counsel for the defence compelled this witness to admit that the great majority of miscarriages are the result of natural causes, and that these are a great many and very varied.

The next witness, Dr. Henry Briggs, who attended with Dr. Paul at the post-mortem examination, agreed with the evidence of Dr. Paul, and clearly stated in answer to a question: "The appearances were consistent with natural miscarriage."

This witness also stated that the slight abrasion could have been caused by the curette used for removing the remainder of the placenta.

After Dr. Briggs' evidence followed that of Dr. John Bligh, the family physician, who said:—

"On the day before Jane Yates' death, I heard of her serious illness at 140 Salisbury Road, and I went there alone the first visit, but subsequently for consultation with Dr. Briggs and Dr. Shaw. I was shown the fœtus, and I agreed that it was about four months old. I formed the opinion that it was dead about a week—any time between three and six days. On the morning of her death, after exchanging views with the two other doctors, I went upstairs and saw Miss Yates. I put some questions to her which she answered, and I embodied her answers in a statement which I read over to

her. I then handed the paper to her and she signed it. She answered somewhat hesitatingly and she knew she was dying. The statement was as
follows:—'*I make this statement in the presence of nurse Rendall and my
sister Miss M. Yates, that I produced the miscarriage myself from the effects
of which I am now suffering, and that I accuse no person of instrumental
interference in its production, and that I have been strongly advised to the
contrary.*—(Signed) JANE YATES, 27th July.'"

This witness continued to describe the discovery of the brown
bag and of the catheter, and stated that he agreed with the other
doctors who attended at the post-mortem examination.

Dr. Hugh T. Shaw, the physician to whom Miss Yates applied
for some medicine to get rid of her trouble, was of the same opinion
as the other doctors, that the miscarriage could have been a natural
one; he went further and said that the probability was that Miss
Yates would have a miscarriage. He also stated that she never
asked him to lend an instrument, as was alleged by the prosecution.

As will be seen hereafter Dr. Shaw's evidence, which was favourable to the prisoner, greatly displeased the presiding judge, who,
in his summing-up, tried to minimise the importance of his statements.

The prosecution laid much stress on the statement which the
prisoner before the inquest had made to a detective, in which he
concealed the fact that he had met Miss Yates at Crewe. The
judge in his *resumé* followed suit, and thereby greatly wronged
the accused. Which man would in a case like this make a truth-
ful statement to a detective? And how could his concealing the
fact of his meeting Miss Yates at Crewe point to his guilt? That
is a question which every reasonable man will ask. It was simply
brought in to increase the prejudice against the victim in the
dock, and it had its effect.

After the witnesses for the prosecution had been heard, Mr.
Gill, counsel for the defence, rose and said:—

I submit, my lord, that the prosecution have not made out a case of
murder. On an indictment for murder what the prosecution have to prove
distinctly is the cause of death, and that applies either to an indictment for
murder or manslaughter. It is absolutely necessary that the prosecution
should establish that death is the result of a felonious act. And where you
have a state of things such as in the present case, where putting the case
for the prosecution at its highest, that the death is consistent with a felonious act or with natural causes, I say there is no case for a jury. I

adopt the view of the prosecution, that the case is one of circumstantial evidence, and that the only direct evidence in the case at all is the dying declaration of the woman herself. That is the only direct evidence admissible, and that does not assist the case for the prosecution. In fact, it is directly opposed to the case for the prosecution. I submit here that it is clearly and abundantly established that the cause of death is consistent with either a felonious act or with natural causes. All the medical witnesses are agreed upon that, and it is not right that a man should be called upon to answer an indictment for murder upon such a condition of facts. The indictment here is directed to a felonious act on the 20th and 21st of July. With regard to that indictment he could only be a principal either in the first or second degree, because the evidence is that he was present in the company of the woman during that time, and it was not possible that he could be found to be accessory before the fact where he was present and in the company of the woman.

THE JUDGE: Is the date material?

MR. GILL: The date is material where the evidence is directed to it.

THE JUDGE: Supposing the jury should be of opinion that it was done on the 22nd—the day after?

MR. GILL: What he is charged with is as principal in the first degree, or as aiding and abetting. I say that you cannot say in a prosecution for murder—"We allege that the murder was the result of a felonious act committed at a particular time over a period of twenty-four hours, that at that time he was principal in the first degree or second degree, if not he was a party to the act which took place sometime either at a later or an earlier date."

THE JUDGE: If you say that the second felony was the cause of death then I am with you. But supposing that on the 20th and 21st all that took place was an arrangement, and that the instrument was actually applied on the 22nd, then could not he be tried on an indictment as accessory before the fact?

MR. GILL: I submit not. It is because I am aware of it that I put forward the argument that a case in which a person can be convicted as accessory before the fact upon an indictment which charges him as principal must be where the evidence goes to show that the felonious act was committed at the particular time alleged, and when the proof falls short, when it is not shown that he was present at it, doing it himself or assisting in the doing of it.

THE JUDGE: I appreciate your point. It is quite worth considering. That is, that if the jury should be of opinion that the felonious act had been committed not on the 20th or 21st, but on the 22nd, he cannot be convicted on this indictment.

MR. PICKFORD: The felonious act was committed on the day of the death.

THE JUDGE: That seems to be the answer.

MR. GILL: Is it that there should be an indefinite charge standing over for a week or a month?

THE JUDGE: That is not what we are dealing with now.

MR. GILL: It is desirable to ascertain what the issues are before the jury.

I say that the prosecution might as well do this—they might as well put forward as their case that death was the result of an act of his done at Crewe; done by him personally, or by the woman in his presence, and say that the evidence failing upon that, he might be accessory before the fact to a distinct act of felony on some other day by the woman herself. If that was so then this kind of case could be made. The prosecution have, themselves, fixed on the 22nd as the date on which they allege this woman used the catheter herself with the intent to procure abortion, and that he was accessory before the fact to it. Instead of charging him with that, suppose they charged him with using the instrument with intent to procure abortion on the 22nd it might be contended—"This is the charge we are making, and we direct our evidence to that, and we say that he used the instrument, or that he was present assisting or that he was accessory before the fact to something that took place somewhere a few days before."

THE JUDGE: You may take it from me, so far, that I shall tell the jury that there is no evidence of any felonious act leading to murder or death prior to the 20th of July. I think any date between the 20th of July and the death might well be covered.

MR. GILL: Wherever he might be? Very well, I have made my submission. I shall have an opportunity of addressing the jury of which I shall avail myself.

THE JUDGE: I think there is a case.

MR. GILL: You think there is a case, my lord?

THE JUDGE: Yes.

As in this remarkable case Judge Phillimore in his summing-up practically acted as prosecutor, and emphasised all the remarks made and arguments brought forward by prosecuting counsel while trying at the same time to belittle or ignore the case for the defence as stated by Mr. Gill, it will be sufficient to give here the speech of the presiding judge and of counsel for the defence to show how successfully, even against the weight of evidence, prejudice can be used against a prisoner guilty of no other offence than that unpardonable sin of so-called immorality.

Mr. Gill rose amid profound silence and said:—

For the first time now since this man was taken into custody, as far back as August 26th of this year, is there an opportunity of saying some word in his defence. This man has from that time up to the time of his committal for trial, and from that time down to the present been in prison, waiting for a period of over three months with this charge hanging over his head; and I am addressing you now on behalf of a man who is broken in health and in fortune, with regard to whom the issue of this case means that he is to go out a ruined man, with a verdict of not guilty, or whether you are to enable the judge, by your verdict, to pass sentence of death upon him. You will, of course, take the law from the judge, but you will realise that you are responsible for the verdict in this case, and that you are the judges of fact here, and that if this man goes from this court condemned to death upon this indictment, it is upon your verdict, and your verdict given upon your personal view of the facts of this case. It was said quite recently by a great judge that there was no better tribunal than a Liverpool jury to deal with questions of fact—far better than any judge. In forming an opinion upon the facts of this case I hope you do not give your judgment away to another man, and that you don't come here to put a construction upon the facts which they do not warrant. You will approach this case with a desire to weigh every fact to see whether a construction could be put upon it hostile to the man in the dock; and you will approach it from the point of view of men desirous to give the man a fair trial, as men mixing with the world and knowing something of the world, and therefore as good judges of fact, and you will look to see where the explanation is that is consistent with innocence. You won't strain your minds to see where you can find material that is consistent with a man's guilt. I beg of you to approach the case from that point of view. You are advanced in life, all of you, and you live in a city where you get great knowledge of the world. And I beg of you to remember that it is your duty personally to exercise your judgment upon the facts of the case, and put your own construction upon them, and not to come into court to put a construction upon them which you might be invited to do, but which might be adverse to the facts. Approach this case as ordinary men of the world, and not as men of ultra-refinement, and bring your ordinary every-day mind to bear upon it. The letters read at the close of the case induce me to make a few observations upon the moral aspects of the case. This is no court of morals. You are not trying this man for immorality. Immorality is no crime. We know that married men have intrigues with women, and that inquiries arise; but don't you, because this man has been immoral, and has been a married man—don't you strain the facts against him from any feeling that you may have upon the question of morality. The place where such things are inquired into is the Divorce Court. Nor is the judge to lecture people on questions of morality. Bear in mind when dealing with these questions that you are not to allow your mind to be influenced hostilely upon the question of morality. Morality is a question of temperament and surroundings. Whatever the character of the prisoner for morality don't exaggerate it. He meets a woman who was not a maiden at the time he met her; immoral relations took place, and he had towards her the strongest possible feeling of affection, as you can gather from the story disclosed in this case over the time that he knew her. You are trying a man whose career has been placed before you from the record of the War Office. Counsel for the prosecution has put his case as strongly as he can, and he has attempted to discount everything that is favourable to the man upon his trial. This man enlists at the age of eighteen and has followed the profession of a soldier. He is on the eve of completing his thirty years' service. He has the highest reputation in the army. He is a man at least deserving of some consideration at your hands, and when you are thinking that he is an immoral man remember that he is a man who has thirty years' barrack-room experience. He has not had a careful education as a boy. He is simply a common, ordinary man commencing life in the way that you now know, and with a career of thirty years as a soldier you should not attach importance to the fact that he writes letters of an indecent character to the woman who is not his wife, but on terms of intimacy with him such as we have had described here. It is not a matter that should affect your minds. What it comes to is this—that a married man, something over forty years of age, who comes to Liverpool as adjutant to a corps of artillery volunteers, and during his time here he meets this woman with whom he became on terms of close intimacy and affection, and with whom immoral relations grew up. He is thrown into contact with her and he yielded to the temptations. What is the case for the prosecution that is presented to you upon this indictment? The case is that you are to find this man guilty of murder because the prosecution say—"We have established to your satisfaction that the prisoner performed a fe.onious operation at Crewe"—not that the case is one of suspicion or anything of that kind—"which operation brought about her death." That is to say that her death was brought about by that operation. And further—"Then, if you are not satisfied with that, our case is that she did it herself, the man being there to assist her to do it, and that that operation brought about the death of the woman." And so he is to be convicted of murder and sentenced to death. Or they say, if you are not satisfied with that—"It may be that he did nothing to her, or that she did nothing to herself at Crewe; but it may be that she herself did perform the operation by passing an instrument into herself," and they say—"if that is so, what we ask the jury to say is that he actively counselled her to do it." That is the case that is before you upon this indictment. You know that there is a bill presented to the grand jury alleging that this woman herself on the 22nd, at Liverpool—

THE JUDGE: I don't think you are entitled to refer to it.

MR. GILL: It has been suggested over and over again in your presence. It is a matter of record here that this man is waiting his trial upon three indictments—indictments quite distinct from this—with being accessory before the fact, on the 22nd. And then the third or last alternative is an indictment charging him with a conspiracy, extending over months, that an illegal operation should be performed upon the woman. All these forms of trial are against this man, who is now being tried upon the first indictment, which is shaped upon the suggestion that the cause of death was the felonious act at Crewe. Why is that? The reason is that you might be strong enough to say that there was no felonious act at Crewe, in the face of the evidence that you have got before you. This shows the absolute uncertainty of the prosecution as to which of those cases should be presented for trial to a petty jury. That is, of course, because of the absence of evidence of any operation at Crewe. But I will only deal with the case upon which you are trying him—that of performing an illegal operation at Crewe. On the question as to whether there was any operation at all at Crewe, what is the evidence? Every circumstance of suspicion has been brought up. What is the evidence from Crewe, beside the evidence of the two servants who saw her on the 20th and 21st? What is the evidence against this man on the charge of murder, for the purpose of satisfying you, as sane men that an operation was performed? It is that she seemed cheerful when she met him—more cheerful than when he left her; and that is put before you as evidence from which to draw some adverse conclusion against this man.

Is the presence of Condy's fluid in the basin a very remarkable thing? That is the whole of the evidence with regard to what took place at Crewe. In that, I submit, there is no element of suspicion that should operate upon your minds. As to the time and place of using the catheter it is all guess-work. You remember the visits to Dr. Shaw, and her being caught in a thunder-storm which terrified her. And it is a remarkable thing that with regard to that thunder-storm that the prisoner, writing after it occurred, speaks of it as being of such a character as likely to terrify her out of her life, and that if she had been there her troubles would have been over. Are prisoners to be tried from the point of view that wherever there is evidence which bears upon their innocence it is to be regarded with suspicion? And that the moment a man says anything in favour of the accused he is to be regarded with the greatest suspicion? Will you do that? Will you ignore everything that is in favour of the prisoner and try to find something of an opposite character? Don't you think she got a severe chill as the result of being caught in that thunder-storm in such a way as to set up trouble with regard to the lungs? What she did on that Friday night we know nothing of. She is out on the Saturday, and on Saturday night she is complaining of a cold, and goes to bed, and she is seen by no one until something like half past ten or eleven o'clock on Monday morning, so that she is left thirty-eight hours without anyone to inquire what her condition was. How do we know what was taking place? You are entirely in the dark with regard to it. It is a lamentable thing that no one was there to help her in that house, so that the subsequent trouble would not have arisen. The next time we find her she is suffering from the effects of a recent miscarriage, carrying a large bag, and wandering about trying to find some place to lay in. She gets to the house of Miss Jackson at two o'clock and she is not seen until half past three by Dr. Shaw. But we do know that she was in a miserable condition when she was seen by Dr. Shaw. Dr. Shaw is dealing with a very strong-willed woman, and she tells him that if he communicates with her mother she would rather kill herself than do that. Dr. Shaw, without calling in other assistance, proceeds to do what he can for her himself. He uses the curette, but he was, unhappily, unable to satisfactorily and completely curette the woman. Portions of the placenta were retained, and that set up inflammation. She got from bad to worse, and Dr. Shaw, finding on Tuesday morning that she was no better, finds it absolutely necessary to communicate with the woman's mother. Then Dr. Briggs is called in, and he finds that it is too late, that nothing can be done. Dr. Bligh is then called in, and he takes her dying statement. Passing from that you come to the post-mortem examination which takes place on the Thursday. I submit to you that where you are trying a man for murder or manslaughter you should not consent under any amount of pressure to give an adverse verdict against a man for causing death unless it is absolutely and clearly proved to you that the cause of death was the result of something done by the man upon his trial. The object of the post-mortem examination is to arrive at the cause of death. The examination results in absolutely no evidence to support the theory of the prosecution that miscarriage was produced by artificial means. What kind of evidence would you expect to find if the abortion was produced by artificial means? It would be of such a character as to point distinctly to its being the result of force used by some instrument, and septicemia would be set up from the wound so caused. Are you going to guess at what is the right construction to put upon the evidence of the doctors, when a man is on trial for his life? There is not only not sufficient evidence, but there is no evidence whatever, because everything is consistent with natural miscarriage. There is nothing in the abrasion which might not very well be caused by the curette.

THE JUDGE: I don't think you need trouble yourself about the abrasion, for it is so extremely probable that it was done by the curette. I shall tell the jury that.

MR. GILL: Eliminate that, and then there is nothing left of the post-mortem examination except that the whole evidence goes to show that the miscarriage was one that would result from natural causes. I say that a man should not be put in peril where the cause of death is proved as consistent with natural causes. If I am right in that view, that it is consistent with natural causes, what do you say to the question as to whether this woman had miscarried naturally? What were the probabilities of her miscarrying naturally? She had been treated by Dr. Bligh for secondary symptoms of syphilis. She was at the time when miscarriage was most likely to occur from natural causes. The result of the post-mortem examination also shows that she had pleurisy and disease of the kidneys. The medical opinion is that the septic pleuritis was the result of blood poisoning from the uterus. When you take the aggregate force of all these matters as an exciting cause—she had met this man recently—is it not highly probable that that miscarriage was not the result of an artificial cause, but of a natural cause? I ask you to take no narrow view of the matter, but to take a broad view of the whole circumstances; and if you do that can you say here that the cause of death was not the result of natural miscarriage? Would you take the responsibility of saying that it could not have been a miscarriage produced by natural means? Any such conclusion would be utterly unsafe. If that is so there is the cause of death, and the case absolutely falls to the ground, and this man is entitled to your verdict in his favour. But what is suggested is that the miscarriage was procured by some felonious act. Having heard the whole story, can you put your finger upon any particular act and say that it was then that the act was committed—perhaps by him, perhaps by her? Perhaps this day or that? That she did it some one or other of those times when they were both together? What importance are you going to attach to the evidence of those experts? When it is adverse to the prisoner are you going to accept it without question, and when it is in his favour are you to reject it? It resolves itself at last into a question of theory. The blood on the catheter—we are entirely in the dark with regard to that. How the blood got on it we know not, and I submit we are not entitled to guess at the cause. The question would arise here of motive. What would be the motive on the part of the prisoner which would make it important to him that this woman should not have a child? There is no reason why he should object to her having a child. There is nothing in his social position to make it a matter of importance to him that she should not have a child. She was a strong-willed woman, and naturally she speaks to and writes to the prisoner with regard to her condition. What is he to do? What is likely to happen is that she may do something. How can you put a construction upon those letters without knowing what the woman wrote to him. His only possible position is to sympathise with her. I submit to you that he was endeavouring to persuade her, if he could, that she must not think of these things, or if she is speaking violently about it, he must temporise. What is the evidence here that he was doing anything more than humouring this woman, pretending that he would help her? Even in the letters that we have heard read you find statements by the prisoner which show what the state of his mind was—that he had no desire that she should procure abortion. These letters show that he was pretending to assist her. In one of them he says :— " I feel I have been in a way unkind in writing despondingly to you, but how is one to get away from writing as they feel; I cannot, sweetheart! You cannot surely mean what you write, when you say or rather accuse me of worrying or funking on my own account. Surely with my love for you I am not justified in risking your life. However unhappy one's life is everyone seems to want to stick to it most tenaciously. If you think that I am thinking only of myself then you do me injustice, and one that most certainly is not by any thought of mine merited. Your life is my life, and one reads so much of the results in such cases that I think one is justified in looking on it with apprehension, or at least with grave danger." That was the state of his mind—in effect, " I'll stick to you forever, but go on with your pregnancy." That shows you what was passing at the time. Bring your knowledge of life and of women to bear on these matters. Try and give a man who has fallen a fair trial even though you are yourself above suspicion. What chance had the man of getting those ideas out of her head. He writes to her :—" I do hope, love, you will decide on allowing things to take their course and face it out. You see, love, nature asserts her rights in spite of all we can do. I do more than mean this." Here is an appeal to her to let things take their course, written on July 10th. On July 14th he writes to her telling her that things must take their course. I say that everything points to the condition that he was simply humouring this woman, and that she suspected he was playing the fool with her, and that she herself attempted to do something when she came back to Liverpool after July 21st. Another matter I would like to bring before you, and it is what I suggest to you is the only piece of direct evidence in the whole of this case. That is the statement of the dying woman. The rest is circumstantial evidence. Do you appreciate what that statement is? I have heard of dying statements being taken against a man upon his trial. But this statement is one which is favourable to the accused, and so it is to be discounted. You are to get over every difficulty, and bridges are to be built for you to escape from accepting anything in favour of this man. But will you do that at the bidding of anyone?—[Counsel here read the statement which has already been given.]—The dying statement clearly and conclusively proves that she in her dying moments denied that anyone had performed an operation upon her, and that she had been strongly advised to the contrary—" that I produced the miscarriage myself from the effects of which I am now suffering." She says, in effect, " if anyone was to blame it was myself." There is the statement of this woman taken under these solemn circumstances, where she almost with her dying breath makes a statement that no person had used an instrument upon her, and bearing in mind, as she would, how time after time she had been advised to the contrary. I submit to you that that has an enormous bearing in this case; and I ask you to take a view of it strongly in favour of the accused; to give it the importance in his favour which you would have to give it if it had contained some accusation against him. As you would give it importance on the other side, so give it importance now that it is in his favour.

Counsel next alluded to the discrepancies in the statements made by the accused to Inspector Gummer, and submitted to the jury that the prisoner had made a mistake at the moment, when he said that he had not seen her for three weeks before her death, whereas the fact was that he had seen her later at Crewe. With regard to that statement (said counsel) the whole tone of it shows that he was answering every question that was put to him, and that there was no desire on his part to deny that he met her at Crewe. He afterwards said that he omitted to state that he had been at Crewe. These are the whole facts of the case; and in the hope that I am addressing gentlemen who will give full weight to the arguments that I have used I press these arguments upon you. I press upon you that the cause of death has not been proved in such a way as to cause you to say that it is the result of a felonious act, and that you cannot say that the miscarriage is not the result of natural causes. Gentlemen, in conclusion, you have the dying statement of the woman herself, and if you return a verdict adverse to this man you will by that verdict of guilty be saying that that dead woman went to face her Maker with a lie upon her lips. I make no comment on the state of the law which makes it possible for a man to be tried for murder on a charge of this kind. I ask you for a fair consideration of this case, and to put aside the question of the prisoner's morality. Judge him as you would desire to be judged yourselves, and if there is amongst you some man of high moral principle who would say that, because a man is immoral, he should be stoned, to such I would say, "Remember that for over three long months this man has been waiting for his trial upon this charge." Can you imagine anything more terrible than for a man to lie down at night, the first and last thought in his mind being that this terrible thing is hanging over him—a charge of murdering the woman he loved best in the world. If you send him as a condemned man from here all his past has gone—the pension which he worked hard to earn. But my last word to you is—Let it be your verdict, let it be the verdict of your judgment. You are the best judges of it; and if you do that I trust to your verdict, and that you will not return an adverse verdict saying that he is guilty on this indictment. —(Applause in court, which was quickly suppressed, the judge warning the public that if he heard anything like it again he would have the court cleared.)

From the summing-up which followed Mr. Gill's speech, it will be seen how Judge Phillimore practically acted as prosecutor in this remarkable case. Guided by his prejudice he traversed one by one the statements made by prisoner's counsel with the sole intention to minimise, to belittle, and even to ignore the points brought out in favour of the acquittal of the accused. It will be observed by impartial readers that the essence of the judge's speech was, that, although there was no proof that an operation had taken place at all, the prisoner must be convicted because he wrote indecent letters to the deceased woman which proved that he was prepared to assist her in an attempt to procure abortion.

THE JUDGE, charging the jury on the whole case, said :—

We are now reaching the end of this case, to which you have given serious attention. I am sure you needed no lecturing upon your duties, and I am quite sure you will not strain your conscience in any way, or strain facts against the prisoner. I exhort you not to do it, and I think the exhortation is quite unnecessary. On the other hand, there is an easy weakness which is criminal. It would be criminal on the part of a jury if they were satisfied that a man was guilty, under the judge's direction on the law, if they let him off upon any ground of hardship, or of his previous good conduct, or any matter of that kind. I have no further general directions to give you. I shall only direct you in matters of law, which you are bound to take from me, and then the facts are wholly for yourself. I shall arrange the facts in the way that seems to me to be the best assistance to you. I shall not read my notes unless you desire it, but if at any time you want any portion of the notes read in full they are here at your service and I shall read them with the greatest pleasure. My direction in the matter of law is this :—The operation of procuring abortion is a felony, and if a person commit it on the body of anyone to whom death thereby results he is guilty of murdering that person. If you intend to beat your enemy within an inch of his life, but not to kill him, but you go beyond that inch and you kill though you never intended to kill, but to do grievous bodily harm, and the man dies the law says that is murder. Another illustration I may give you. Very early in my judicial career I had to try a very shocking case where death was produced by an act of rape. The man didn't intend to kill the woman. He used no other violence to her except that. She was an old woman, and the act of forcible sexual intercourse killed her. I directed the jury that if they found that the act killed the woman they should find the man guilty of murder, and the jury loyally conformed to my direction. If the prisoner did procure abortion on the person of Jane Yates, and if the consequence of that abortion was her death, he is guilty of murder. Now, the second proposition—If the unfortunate woman caused her own miscarriage, then, as far as she is concerned, it was in law a case of suicide or *felo de se.* And if in this last case the prisoner was her accomplice, and aided and abetted an illegal operation which caused her death, though he did not put the instrument into her womb, he is equally responsible for her death, and he is guilty of murder. If he in any way, however slight, assisted in the operation and encouraged it by, for instance, getting the room for it to take place in—in that case he would be principal in the second degree. The third proposition is—If he merely counselled or helped the operation, and was not present at it, he would be accessory before the fact, and would be still guilty of murder. The text-books give an example :—"A man counselling a woman to murder her child when it should be born, and she murdered it accordingly, was therefore held to be accessory before the fact." In the first place—Was an illegal operation performed upon this woman with a view to producing miscarriage? Second—Did the prisoner do the operation or help in its being done?—it matters not which. And, third—Did the woman die of the results of this illegal operation? If the answer is Yes to each of these three questions the prisoner is guilty of murder. If No to any one of the three he is not guilty. There is no doubt that Jane Yates is dead. There is no doubt that she had a miscarriage, and I take it, there is no doubt that miscarriage caused her death. This leaves you only to consider two questions—Was the miscarriage artificial and illegal, or was it natural, and, consequently, had the prisoner no share in it in the way I have already explained to you? Mr. Gill, in his defence, has made the point, more than once I think, in the course of the case that there are other indictments on the file against this prisoner, and it is true that there are other two. But I have considered these more than once, and I may tell you that as at present advised if you return a verdict of not guilty in this case there is but one contingency on which the prisoner could be tried upon anything else. I wish to say that he is not being tried upon anything else except this one contingency. If— and it has been suggested by Mr. Gill—it should turn out to be the truth that he had not counselled this woman to procure miscarriage, and that he never intended or tried to do it, but that, in fact, the miscarriage was a natural miscarriage, then he would not be guilty of murder, because it would not be her act or his that led to her death. It would be natural miscarriage, and in that case only would it be possible to try him upon another charge. One other preliminary matter. Something has been said as to the character of this man. Gentlemen, in a case of this kind not too much weight should be attached to good or bad character. It is not a case where, with the admitted goodness or the admitted badness of the prisoner's character, we can infer very much as to the probability of his not doing or doing this act. We know that he is a very meritorious soldier who has risen from the ranks, although he seems to lack somewhat in the matter of morality. On the other hand, we unfortunately know that being now of the age of 48—having come to Liverpool in 1892 at the age of 40, when the girl was just 21—he very soon entered into intimate acquaintance with her, which ripened as far back as the year 1890, when he was 42 and she about 23—and intercourse has taken place ever since—beginning, in fact, when she was in a sense his pupil. It may be that he was not her original seducer. There is a doggerel rhyme addressed by him to her in which he suggests that she was not a maiden when he met her, and as she kept and treasured all those letters one may assume that she did not resent the statement. But however that may be he got to know this girl when she was but 21, and at 23 he began immoral relations with her. And we also know from the correspondence, which unfortunately it was our duty to read, that the intercourse has been of the most offence and gross description, and that they have not hesitated to recall the grossest of the acts which took place. I don't know. It is for you to say whether from that you would infer that a man was likely or not likely to stick at getting rid of the embodiment of shame to the girl. That is all we can say about that matter. Now, there is no doubt the girl is dead,

and dead by reason of blood-poisoning due to miscarriage, and as I understand the doctors that blood-poisoning may have arisen in one of two ways.
With every miscarriage there is some danger—I mean with every delivery
in due course there is some danger of a portion of some membrane remaining
in the womb which rots, and which if it remains in the womb will set up
mischief, and may set up poison, or may slough itself away. It may be
relieved by the mere process of syringing, it may be relieved by the use of
the finger if a medical operator is at hand shortly after the event, and when
the orifice is wide. Or by the curette, afterwards inserted into the womb.
Therefore it may be that some of the afterbirth did not come away, and if
you add to that the condition of a woman with some ancient syphilitic
symptoms you can understand that the afterbirth would be more offensive
than it otherwise would be. A family man who has ever had anything to do
with a matter of that kind may know that a doctor is very particular in
such matters, but if an artificial miscarriage, produced by a catheter, used
by an unskilled operator, takes place there is great danger. If it is properly
and skilfully handled it may do no mischief as it goes in. The idea is that
it remains there as a kind of foreign substance, that it sets up muscular
irritation of the womb and thus expels the fœtus. If properly and carefully inserted it may do no damage in the shape of tearing or cutting, but if
it is not clean it may carry with it some germ of disease; and, again, being
hollow, it may suck up the air and various impurities which might create
blood-poisoning. Therefore, with the use of the catheter you have great
danger of producing blood-poisoning; and one may say that the common
danger is more common in this case, for in such a case as this one is not
likely to go to a medical man, and as a consequence a portion of the afterbirth
may remain. Mr. Gill has said with considerable insistence that you ought
not to find a verdict against this man when the post-mortem signs do not
tell you for certain that the abortion was one of natural character. If that
were so numbers of abortionists would escape, because the doctors tell us
that in many cases of carefully procured miscarriage it is impossible to tell
after death whether the miscarriage was artificial or natural. All that they
can say is that the symptoms are neutral, pointing neither way, and if there
is no other evidence the jury must acquit the prisoner. But it does not
negative any other evidence that there is. For instance—to give you a
rough illustration. A man is found dead with his throat cut; that is consistent with suicide or murder. If you find nothing else the coroner's jury
brings in an open verdict. But if you find strong reasons for supposing that
A.B. was the murderer you don't let A.B. go scot free because on the post-
mortem alone you cannot tell whether it was murder or suicide. But other
evidence comes in and says it is murder. Here in this case the post-mortem
simply says that the woman died of blood-poisoning due to miscarriage. But
they don't show to us whether it was artificial or natural, and if you rest
upon that alone you can go no further. Let us approach that question. Did
she desire an artificial miscarriage? Did she take steps to procure it? Did
she succeed or did she fail? Had she a natural pre-disposition to natural
miscarriage? One of three views is apparently presented to you for your
consideration—one, that she never interfered with herself at all, and that
the miscarriage was wholly natural; secondly, that she interfered with her-

self, but did not succeed, and that the thing was natural; and, thirdly, that it was brought about by artificial means with or without the help of the prisoner. I think it is convenient here to read over portion of the evidence of doctors which bears upon this part of the case, and then we will clear the medical evidence away. The first was Dr. Paul who says the woman died of septic peritonitis, or blood-poisoning. He made a post-mortem examination, and the result of his observations was that he could not say whether it was a natural miscarriage or not. He says:—"There was nothing to show whether it was a natural miscarriage, or one that had been brought on by an operation." There are, of course, rough artificial abortions, done with knitting needles or pieces of wire, by opening some orifice and so bringing about premature delivery; but the suggestion here is that this was a carefully and very skilfully contrived operation by the use of this (catheter) comparatively soft and flexible instrument in such a manner as not to injure the parts. I advise you not to attach any importance to that small abrasion in the womb. It is quite likely that it is due to the operation of curetting afterwards. I advise you also to reject that and accept to the full Dr. Paul's evidence when he says that there is nothing to show you whether she died of artificially produced or natural miscarriage. He says:—"The fœtus was quite four months old." That is important to remember, for it appears to be common ground that the later you get the more improbable natural abortion is.—[His lordship here read his notes of the cross-examination of Dr. Paul, which need not be repeated, and then he read the evidence of Drs. Briggs and Bligh.]—The next witness and the most important in some respects (continues his lordship) is Dr. Shaw, and I must say that I am not at all satisfied with some portion of his evidence. He says she came to see him on the 22nd to ask if he was going away on his holidays. She made no request of him then, but she had been with him some time previously and asked for some medicine to get her out of her trouble. He, of course, refused it. There was never any request made to him for an instrument, although it is suggested in a letter by the prisoner. He says:—"I thought it may be possible that she may abort naturally." The only other evidence on this point is that of the girl's mother. The mother says she left home on Wednesday the 20th July, the week before she died, and did not return until 8 o'clock on the night of the following day. On Friday the 22nd she went out at 4 o'clock in the afternoon, and did not return until 7 o'clock, or a little later, and while she was out she was caught in a thunder-storm. On the next day, Saturday, she went to bed about 9 o'clock in the evening, and stayed in bed all day on Sunday. On Monday morning she came downstairs and left the house about half past eleven o'clock, carrying with her the brown bag, so frequently referred to. Gentlemen, it is for you to consider whether it was due to lassitude after excessive sexual intercourse and the travelling that she lay in bed, or whether she was lying up for the purpose of using the catheter. There, you have all the medical evidence on the question as to whether this miscarriage was natural or artificial. I don't think it has much bearing on it but I will mention it, that Miss Jackson said when Jane Yates arrived at her house there was blood issuing from the womb. She is said to have some syphilitic tendency, and that is said to have some tendency to abortion. It is said, on the other hand, that she might have been frightened by the thunder. Then we know that she desired miscarriage, and Dr. Shaw says she was likely to abort naturally. On the other hand, you have the fact that she had no illness likely to cause abortion. But now we have a great amount of other material upon this subject. We have, first of all, her own statement. It is got by question and answer, and it is taken down by the doctor in some hurried way. But it is the impression produced upon his mind and he wrote it down. (Statement read by his lordship.) Mr. Gill has elicited from Dr. Bligh that he asked her positively if anyone had used an instrument upon her, and that she denied it, and said that if anyone was to blame it was herself. Gentlemen, it is for you to say whether this is consistent with a natural miscarriage. If you think that this woman tried once, twice, and thrice to produce miscarriage you will probably be slow to think that her own action was the cause of it. Now as to the question of this man's complicity. Take her dying statement in its strongest form. She was asked by Dr. Bligh if anyone had used an instrument upon her, and she said "No." Great weight should, no doubt, be attached to that. I offer only two considerations for you with respect to it. The first is that that does not absolve the prisoner, because it may be perfectly consistent with the fact that she used the instrument herself, and yet he may be standing by aiding and abetting. That does not absolve the prisoner if you believe what took place on the 20th and 21st in the room in Crewe. And the other observation I would make is this—it is quite true that it is an awful thing for anybody to meet his last end with a lie on his lips. But there are lies and lies, and if this woman was attached to this man, and if any good purpose was to be served, in her judgment, by not putting it on him, one can conceive that her love might have been quite strong enough for her to say: "I will take the blame of all this upon myself." His lordship next read the statement of the prisoner to the detective officer, and referred particularly to this clause:—"About three months ago Miss Yates informed me that she was pregnant, and asked what was best to be done," and "I have no knowledge of any operation performed upon her." If that statement is true, on the whole case he had nothing to fear except the dreadful exposure of this case. But unfortunately there is one item in that part of the statement which is not correct:—"The last time I saw Miss Yates alive was in London three weeks before her death." That is incorrect, for the last time he saw her was at Crewe six or seven days before her death. The detective had information evidently which led him to think that the meeting had been in London, and he asked him if he met her on the 20th and 21st in London, and he said:—"No, the last time I met her was three weeks before her death." It may be that he was led off the track by the suggestion of London. On the other hand, he may be desirous of leading the detective off the track. Did the prisoner intend to deceive, and if so was it with the intention of concealing their meeting at Crewe? (His lordship here read his notes of the evidence of the witnesses from Crewe.) Continuing he said:—I agree with Mr. Gill that the evidence of the hotel attendants at Crewe was of the smallest description, and hardly worth considering as evidence in the case. It came only to this—that she looked happy when he came to meet her, and unhappy when he went away. But what we are considering are the letters which passed from him to her. You have had only one letter from her to him. I have on my own responsibility excluded a letter which she did not send, because I consider that a statement not made on oath ought not to be used against the prisoner. The letter which I admitted was portion of the correspondence. We have had none of the earlier letters—whether he kept them, or whether he destroyed them before or after this trouble we know not. They might throw some light upon his letters back to her. Nor have we that letter, the last which he wrote to her, which he claimed at the house of call and destroyed. The first letter which we have had before us is the letter of May 23rd, in which he writes:—"My darling crystal, I feel I have been in a way unkind to you in writing despondently to you, but how is one to get away from writing as they feel; I cannot, sweetheart! You cannot surely mean what you write, when you say or rather accuse me of worrying or funking on my own account. Surely with my love for you I am not justified in risking your life. However unhappy one's life is everyone seems to want to stick to it most tenaciously. If you think that I am thinking only of myself then you do me an injustice, and one that most certainly is not by any thought of mine merited. Your life is my life, and one reads so much of the results (fatal) in such cases that I think one is justified in looking on it with apprehension, or at least with grave danger. You need not have told me that you would not give me away knowingly. I have felt all that long long ago, and I am pleased to say that the feeling is more than reciprocated. Not that your doing so could make the smallest difference. See, love! If you are looking forward to the 6th of June for any righting of our wrongs, eliminate the notion at once, love. Oh, no, I most certainly do not! As you experienced unusual pleasure it must necessarily be neutralised by an unusual amount of pain, which I very much regret I cannot bear myself instead of you." There is no doubt (said the judge) that at one time this unfortunate man did try to dissuade this woman from doing this act. Can anyone doubt after reading these letters that at one time there was a discussion between them as to some intention or means of procuring abortion. She has suggested some form of abortion and he complains of it. In the letter of June 22nd he writes:—"Well then, love, as to S. (that is, Dr. Shaw), I fancy you will find him obdurate, and without flesh in his heart, which he most certainly is to refuse anything such a sweet, pleading face might ask." Then in the letter of the following day, June 23rd, he writes:—"So the sooner we arrange a meeting the better. 'You don't know how you will get away, love.' What price me! Of course, I am free from Saturday afternoon till Monday morning. But what is troubling me is sending you away from me apprehending what may happen. I am aware of your inimitable pluck and capability of enduring pain, but would much prefer it to be endured with me, as I have a sort of feeling that I could mitigate it to some extent." In another letter he writes:—"You write as though you were in dread of my not complying with your request. But I have done my very best and will do so again. But you, for some reason or other, of pain or something, when I moved my fingers began to twitch your stomach." It has been suggested that he was putting her off. But how are we to get rid of that record of something having been done which was ineffectual? The disgusting suggestion that she could cover her shame by marrying another man was discussed

several times in the course of these letters, and in one of them (June 22nd)
you will find a most horrible suggestion with regard to the woman's sister.
It is suggested that if she married this man (G.) she could get him (prisoner)
an introduction to her own sister for the purpose of sexual intercourse. For
what purpose was the meeting arranged which has been referred to in the
letter of June 23rd? There was something to happen which would cause
her pain, and which would probably last longer than from Saturday to
Monday, and he proposes a meeting when they could have a longer time
together. In the letter of June 29th he writes:—"I shall come down to
see you on Saturday evening same time as last time if possible, when you
slated me soundly for coming, or rather not coming, by the train before.
I think it starts at 5.30. Of course, love, shall have to return on Sunday
evening. If I can possibly arrange to come on Friday evening I shall wire
you to-morrow. Must wire you now or you will kill me. Perhaps Ma smells
a —— as to your condition.   She ought to know something about such
things. Those breasts of mine are sure to give me away; or perhaps it is
that she has discovered those cataracts and twigs your little game." In the
same letter he writes:—" Mind you bring all the implements. So now, love,
Friday if possible, and Saturday possible or not.   I think that is clear."
Then there is a discussion about money. What did they want money for?
Was it to go away? It is fair to the man to say that at this time he was
unwilling to go any further. But does he not admit in this letter that he
has already gone some distance. In the letter dated July 10th (according
to the post-mark on the envelope) he writes:—" I am living in the fond hope
of having some better news from you to-morrow. But fate seems horribly
against us, love. Why didn't S. keep his promise, the idiot? Yes, love,
I shall try my best to get hold of the mysterious letter, but I fear there is
but small hope. . . . I do hope, love, that you will decide on letting
things take their course and face it out. You see, love, nature seems to
assert its rights this time in spite of all we can do." Then there is the
letter of July 12th in which he says:—" I can manage to get down as far
as Crewe, where you will have to manage to meet me, if only for an hour.
I cannot possibly get leave, so I will have to get down and return the same
day, unless, as you most unkindly put it, pinky rights herself in the mean-
time, when you wouldn't have to trouble me. Heavens, trouble me! That
is good, awfully." In a postscript in this letter he writes:—"Sweetheart,
that is the best I can do for you at present, and if we fail this time, well,
then, what's to be done? I don't know. Kick the bucket, I suppose, which
seems to me to be far the easiest thing to do." What I understand by that
(said his lordship) is:—" I'll go unless you have got the miscarriage before
that date." And again he says:—" I think it best to do it now as there
is some little show going on "—"show" meaning that there was a show of
blood, and that that was the time to do it. "I wonder it did not occur to
you to remove the 'cat,' by keeping it a bit aided by 'Pimple's' medicine "—
that is to say (says the judge) helping the action of the womb by some medicine which assists abortion. In a postscript he writes:—"I wish I could
get one of those other things but S. would not lend it." The woman was
so firm in her pregnancy that nothing will bring about the miscarriage.
There is a letter dated July 15th in which he writes:—"However 'All's

well that ends well,' but our trouble is not ended now, just yet. I own to presentiments of its ending far from well for us. However, it shall be all just as you wish it, love. I know you mean it all for the best, and I sincerely hope it will turn out so. But I do wish to my heart it may be averted by any honourable means. I hope to hear by letter in the morning that you have arranged something. I am horribly upset. I don't wish anyone any harm, but S. I hope will want something done for him as badly as we do now, the frightened idiot." All these circumstances, gentlemen, you will have to consider, and come to the best conclusion you can upon them. The matter is now ready for you to deal with. The Crown says that this took place on the 20th or 21st of July when the two people were together at Crewe. It is quite true that there is no direct evidence of what happened. There were only two people present, and one of them is dead, the other is in the dock. Therefore the best evidence that you can get is circumstantial evidence; but circumstantial evidence may be distrusted when it is put in the place of direct evidence. But where there is no direct evidence, as in many criminal cases, you must depend upon circumstantial evidence. If you are of opinion that more than once before, these persons had tried artificial means to procure miscarriage, and that they met on this occasion with a view to doing it, and if you find that shortly afterwards the woman had a miscarriage, then it is open to you to say, and it would be right for you to say, if you believe it, that the miscarriage was effected when these two people met together. As I said before, it is for the purposes of this trial quite immaterial whether the man inserted the instrument into the body of the woman, or whether he stood by assisting or counselling or encouraging it. It may be that if you feel it your duty to return a verdict against this man those matters would be very properly considered by those who have the prerogative of mercy. But for the purposes of the law it matters not whether the man performed the operation or the woman herself did it with the man standing by. It is possible that it was not done till a later date— till she had seen Dr. Shaw. It may have been done, says counsel for the prisoner, after she had seen Dr. Shaw that Friday night. It might have been done on the Saturday though she was out most of that day, and it might have been done on the Sunday, and the thing might have come away on Monday. All I have to say with regard to this is that the main case for the Crown is that it was done on the 20th or 21st. If you think that it was done at a later date by the woman, and that it was done by her, because the man, though absent, advised her to do it, then he is as responsible for her doing it two days afterwards as if it was done in his presence. Gentlemen, you have now the whole matter before you. I am sorry to have detained you so long. I'll ask you to take this bundle of letters, and to consider your verdict.

After an absence of an hour and a half the jury returned into court at a quarter past nine o'clock with a verdict of guilty of murder, to which they added a strong recommendation to mercy.

THE CLERK: Prisoner, you have been found guilty of murder, have you anything to say why sentence should not be pronounced upon you, according to law?

THE PRISONER, pulling himself erect in soldierly fashion, and firmly clutching the taffrail of the dock in front of him, answered:—

No, my lord, except that I am innocent. I wish to say that the statement made by the deceased lady was absolutely true, and that that made by myself also was absolutely true with the exception that I should have said that the last time I saw the lady alive was three weeks before. That is wrong, but through no fault of mine. The suggestion was made by the detective from London. He said to me:—"It is suggested that you were in London on such and such a date," to which I replied:—"That is wrong; I was not." But it has been put in a different form. I never said such a thing. One thing more I would like to say, and that is, my lord, that there are perhaps few men who would like to have the worst portion of their lives laid bare before the British public; and no doubt many will criticise my writing and think that the deceased lady corresponded with me in a similar way. I am pleased to be able to say that in the seven years I knew her and corresponded with her she never once made use of an immodest expression or wrote an immodest word, and because I chose to stick to her like a man I am here now for it. Had I thrown her on one side like a child tired of its toys—but having known her as I did my wife—all would have been well. The letters have been cruelly misinterpreted and wrongly, and I could tell you a story that would show you that it is absolutely true beyond any dispute. The letters, to begin with, are put all in the wrong place. They have no dates as is well known to your lordship, and although they have been made by manipulation to look to have a succession of running, it is not so; and there are several of those letters which do not belong to either of the months that are shown. I would like to say a very great deal, my lord, but under the circumstances, and after the length of time the jury have been occupied, I will say no more beyond thanking your lordship and the gentlemen of the jury for the very attentive hearing they have given to my painful case. I wish also to thank Mr. Gill for his inimitable defence of my innocence, and I would like to add that there have been a number of letters kept back that would have proved my innocence beyond doubt. The Scripture says, my lord, "Cursed be he who removeth his neighbour's landmark," and I say, my lord, that thrice cursed be he or she who keeps back evidence wilfully that would prove a man's innocence. That, my lord, has been done, and if things will happen in the end as I hope they will, your lordship will know that I stand in front of you now an innocent man.

A VOICE IN COURT: Hear, hear.

THE PRISONER: It is due to the girl's mother to say that she did all a woman could do to stop the intrigue at the time it first started, and it is also due to my wife, who is not here, to say that she did all she could. Of her I will speak as the best wife and the best mother of children that God ever gave to man; but when she found she could not stop the intrigue, like the good woman she is, she held her tongue, hoping that one day I would turn from my wickedness and sins. But, my lord, having won the girl's love and taught her to love me with her heart and soul, and to place implicit confidence and a child's simple trust in me, how could I throw her on one side, having known her as I did? No, I stuck to her to the bitter end, and it is no fault of mine that she did not die in the arms of the man she loved. I was making my way to her, and it is no fault of mine that I was not there. There have been letters innumerable, and it is almost enough to make a man turn away from God's holy book to know that anyone can go into the box there and kiss the book and tell your lordship and the gentlemen of the jury the lies they have told. I am now at your mercy, my lord.

MR. JUSTICE PHILLIMORE, addressing the prisoner, who remained standing in the dock, said:—

Robert John Wark, the jury have found you guilty of murder. They have found that you were a party to procuring the abortion of this woman, which abortion ended in her death, and I do not think, as the law stands, that they could properly have found otherwise. They have strongly recommended you to mercy. That strong recommendation shall be my care, and shall be duly forwarded to the proper quarter. What the result may be I do not know. It may be that you will be reprieved, and it may be that you will not. My duty now is to pass upon you the sentence of the law, and to urge upon you to remember, whether your period of probation on earth be short or long, that you have much to repent of, and I hope you will employ that time to advantage.

Sentence of death in the prescribed form was then passed upon the prisoner, who listened to it with remarkable imperturbability, the only sign of emotion which he displayed being a slight twitching of his face when he heard the solemn words pronounced. At the conclusion of the painful scene the prisoner whose military bearing did not desert him even in this trying ordeal, turned round, and with a nod of recognition to some persons in the gallery, disappeared into the cells below.

What happened after this extraordinary outrage to justice? A murmur of indignation ran through the court, and a crowd soon assembled outside, which cheered Lieutenant Wark who, after receiving his death sentence, was being conveyed back to gaol. The public conscience must have been aroused in a high degree to produce such an unheard-of demonstration after a murder trial. The cry of indignation went forth and was carried all over England, it found an echo in every town and village of the vast empire.

No doubt, soon after the sentence, the judge himself became conscious of the serious blunder, and the Home Secretary acted promptly in reprieving the unfortunate officer. Within a few days the death sentence was commuted into one of three years' penal servitude.

This half-hearted measure to repair a great wrong could not fail to accentuate the scandal, and a well-known weekly expressed the opinion of lawyers on the subject as follows:—

"There has seldom been a clearer case of undue influence on the part of the Bench; and since there is practically unanimity on the part of the Bar that there never was sufficient evidence to warrant the case going to a jury, it is difficult to see by what process of reasoning the Home Secretary has arrived at the conclusion that the prisoner was guilty, but only sufficiently guilty to merit half the sentence imposed on Dr. Collins, and one quarter of that imposed on Dr. Whitmarsh. Either the crime was committed, and deserved at least the former of these two punishments, or else, as some of the keenest intellects in England, both legal and lay, believe, the prisoner is entirely guiltless, and has already suffered irreparable injury. In deference to this opinion, the sentence has been merely watered down on the theory that a man's guilt is only half condoned if it be only half proved."

Another influential journal said:—

"No Cadi of an Eastern Court ever committed a grosser injustice than that which disgraced our country when Lieutenant Wark was sent to penal servitude."

As usual the sycophantic press, more or less, hushed the case up for fear that the foreign, and especially the French, press could take hold of it, but a courageous article in the old *Westminster Review* should here be mentioned as giving an explanation of the psychological basis of this and similar decisions which offend the public conscience. The *Westminster Review* says:—

"It was proved beyond a shadow of doubt that the man took a manly and praiseworthy view of his responsibilities; that he was prepared to act up to those responsibilities in the fullest sense; that he might, if he had adopted the callous attitude of the mere sensualist, have reduced those responsibilities to a ridiculous minimum, and kept himself free from any of the risks that overtook him, leaving the woman to take care of herself; and that he did his utmost to dissuade her from having recourse to any illegal act. That he was in any sense a participator in that act there was no direct evidence to show, while the solemn declaration made by the woman when she was dying absolved him from all responsibility. No doubt it may be argued that that declaration might have been influenced by the woman's regard for her lover; but against that there is the peculiar solemnity attached by the law, and properly attached, to a declaration made in the immediate anticipation of death. In spite of all these facts, however, the remorseless theory of constructive murder was dragged in; the woman's dying declaration was, by direction of the judge, practically disregarded; and the prisoner had to submit to the pain and stigma of a capital sentence which everyone in the court knew would never be carried out.

"It is not difficult to understand what it was that shocked public feeling, what it was that led to the extraordinary demonstration of sympathy that took place when the sentenced man was being conveyed back to prison. That the law itself—the law that inflicted a capital sentence under conditions which would not suffer such a sentence to be carried out—was wrong was plain enough. This fact alone would tend to create sympathy with the recipient of such a sentence. Further than this, there was the absence of direct evidence against the prisoner, and the apparent determination of the judge to secure a conviction in spite of such absence of direct evidence. Further even than this, there was the disregard shown for the dying declaration of the woman whose life had been sacrificed—a disregard seen to be all the more striking when contrasted with the straining against the prisoner of the dying declaration of the victim in the Whitmarsh case. But even more powerful than these suggestions to sympathy was the fact, abundantly clear to the mind of every man present, that if the prisoner, callously ignoring his responsibilities, had played the part of a mere sensualist, he could never have been placed in such jeopardy. It thus became apparent that the law, as administered in the Liverpool Assize Court, was being converted into an agent for the encouragement of selfish sensuality, and for the discouragement of the manliness which declines to shrink from just responsibilities. To put it briefly, the lesson taught in the Liverpool Assize Court was this: 'We cannot punish men for their irregular relations with women. We warn them, however, in their own interest, to keep those irregular relations down to the level of mere brutal sensuality, to allow them to be affected by no sense of sincere affection, to be callous as to any responsibilities that they may create, and to thrust off into the gutter any woman who is inconsiderate enough to become pregnant. If they follow this course, their days shall be long in the land, and their reputations shall shine untarnished. If they are so humane and so manly that they decline to follow this course, then we shall hang them if we possibly can, and in any case condemn them to the lingering degradation of a long term of penal servitude.'

"Is there any need to marvel at the sympathy expressed for the prisoner at Liverpool as he was conveyed from the Assize Court back to the gaol from which, if his sentence was carried into effect, he would never come out alive? The Anglo-Saxon sense of justice, moral as well as legal, was in revolt, and men would have been false to themselves if they had failed to express that sympathy."

. . . .

"It is easy to argue that if there were no sexual irregularity—if all men could be rendered unselfish and all women rendered less weak—there would be no necessity for discussing such a problem as this. It is, however, impossible to get rid of sexual irregularities. They always have had, and always will have, their existence. What we have to do is to find out how they can be prevented from leading to more serious evils—such evils, for example, as the wholesale desire for, and practice of, infanticide. That class distinction has much to do with the creation of such irregularities there can be no doubt. Where there is an equality of social level irregularities are not nearly so liable to occur, or, if occurring, do not lead to such disastrous results. Men belonging to the upper classes do not as a rule prey upon the women of their own class. They are restrained either by the sense of honour or by fear of the consequences. Among the rural population such irregularities more often than not lead to marriage—a fact which shows that, though the ideal of marriage is not the highest, there is yet an ideal of a sort. It is the liability of the woman of a lower class to be flattered by the attentions of the man of a class above her that is most frequently responsible for sexual irregularities. This is the popular conviction on the subject, and the conviction is substantially justified by facts. And on whom does the blame rest in these cases? Public opinion has not unfrequently been ready to lay all the blame upon the ' dissolute man ' of Hood's ' Bridge of Sighs.' There may be justice in that view; and yet, strange to say, while public opinion is ready to lay all the blame upon the man, both law and public opinion lay all the punishment upon the woman. The selfish, sensual, dissolute man is not only subjected to no kind of moral stigma, but can escape from all legal responsibility, if the victim of his sensuality should become a mother, by the payment of a sum so trifling as to be ridiculous. To the woman, if her giving way to sexual irregularity becomes known, the punishment, if not death itself, is one that may very well seem worse than death. No one can pretend to call this justice; while, to make the injustice greater, the punishment inflicted upon the woman, and some part of which she may possibly deserve, is extended, if she should become a mother, to her innocent children.

" Arrived at this point, it seems impossible not to stand aghast, not only at the injustice inflicted upon women, but at the terrible carelessness of the law as to the fate of children. All the punishment for having evolved an illegitimate child, and all the responsibility for that child's future, are thrown upon the woman. The law absolves the father from responsibility; the State refuses to take any responsibility upon itself. It is upon the mother, banned by public opinion, disabled by being thus banned from engaging in any decent occupation, utterly repudiated in the vast majority of cases by her own kith and kin—it is upon this unhappy mother that the sole responsibility is thrust for the well-being and bringing up of her child. Can any reasonable person marvel that a woman, weak and offending though she may have been, should seek to escape from a position of such inhuman injustice by compassing the destruction of her offspring before it is born? Let any happy and self-respecting woman, herself the rejoicing mother of children, try to put herself in the place of a mother-to-be who has not gone through the ceremony of marriage. The fear of detection; the certainty of reprobation; the almost certain repudiation by her relatives; her possible desertion by the man who has been her lover; the prospect of a new life to be somehow provided for by means, perhaps, from which her whole nature revolts—can it be possible to place a more terrible burden upon any human creature? And yet, so extraordinarily powerful are the instincts of nature, that beneath all this accumulation of torment and injustice the sense of maternal affection and solicitude persists—persists with such force that even if the worst comes to the worst, and the welfare of the child can only be secured by acceptance of the hire of the harlot, the mother is morally redeemed in spite of her surroundings.

" The cruelty inflicted upon the mother, the injustice which suffers the father to escape practically scot-free, these are parallelled by the criminal carelessness of the State as to the future of the children who spring from irregular unions. One would think, having regard to this carelessness, that the State, which undertakes to punish infanticide, merely wished to encourage it. Children thus born, with everything against them, might reasonably be regarded as, and not improbably are, the material from which the criminal class are recruited. The State, however, takes no pains to provide against such a probable contingency. Such children belong to nobody except to their mothers, and their mothers, by the common consent of law and public opinion, are practically debarred from giving them a chance in life. Is it not to the interest of the State, is it not to the interest of society, that such children should be put out of the way? The State, in its profound inconsistency, says 'No': yet it will not move a finger to compel the father of the illegitimate child to recognise the responsibility which is his quite as much as the mother's, if not more. Logically speaking, the child that is born subject to the disadvantage of illegitimacy should have more care bestowed upon it than is bestowed upon children who are legitimate. The popular argument against that is, of course, that to improve the status of illegitimate children would be to give encouragement to sexual irregularity. It would, however, be difficult to increase the encouragement which, so far as men are concerned, exists already; while there can be little doubt that a considerable diminution of encouragement would result if the State, undertaking, if only in its own defence, the charge of illegitimate children, were to insist on being recouped by the parents who are best able to pay.

"But, after all is said, there is one compelling force to the crime of infanticide which is, perhaps, more powerful than any other. Grant that it is by the 'dissolute man' that so many women are betrayed away from the path of virtue. Grant this; but then go on to admit that it is by the pitiless woman that they are prevented from rescuing themselves. The sentence of ostracism against the woman who, whether through her own weakness or as the victim of fraud, once steps off the narrow path is unalterable. It does not matter, in the general opinion of women, whether her sin is accidental or a trade. She is to be shunned and reprobated; there is no forgiveness for her. Every woman knows this, and it is more because of this than anything else that women, possessed often of admirable qualities, but who have been too generous in the bestowal of their affection, are, sooner than face the perpetual scorn of their own sex, tempted to the adoption of criminal means of escape. Let the women who draw their skirts around them to avoid contact with vice remember this—that if the sin which was accidental becomes a trade, it is, in ninety-nine cases out of a hundred, because the women who have never been tempted refuse the hand of help to those who have yielded to temptation. There is no woman who enters on a career of professional vice willingly; there are few women who, having entered on such a career, would not give more than all they possess to be able to escape from it. They might have escaped if only their own sex had helped them in the first instance; as their own sex held aloof, they have had to choose between starvation and the profession of vice. It is no use for those who have driven their less fortunate sisters into the gutter to come afterwards and try to pick them out again with a long pair of theological tongs. What is wanted is that individual charity and help from the strong woman to the weak which alone can make effective the impulse towards self-redemption. When this exists as the rule, and ceases to be the exception, we shall have done with infanticide."

No legal remedy against this outrage on law and justice being available a petition was addressed to the Home Secretary. The document, which was of a most bulky and weighty character, was signed by over two hundred justices of the peace, barristers, and solicitors, by over 12,000 journalists, architects, and professional men, by more than 30,000 artizans, soldiers, and sailors, and by about 6,000 inhabitants of Liverpool. The majority of about 50,000 signatures were obtained by the prisoner's friends in Woolwich. The petition ran as follows:—

"To the Right Hon. Sir Matthew White Ridley, Bart., M.P., her Majesty's Principal Secretary of State for the Home Department.

"The humble memorial of the undersigned

"Showeth

"That Robert John Wark, aged forty-six, was on Thursday, the 8th day of December, found guilty at the Liverpool Assizes of the murder of Jane Yates, was sentenced to death, and has since been reprieved. The prisoner is at her Majesty's Prison, Walton.

"That your memorialists have read and considered the evidence adduced at the trial.

"That the only direct evidence in the case distinctly negatived the performance of any operation by the prisoner on the deceased, and further proved that the prisoner did not counsel or procure the performance of such operation; on the other hand, there was evidence that the prisoner had strongly advised the deceased not to commit or permit an unlawful act, but to let nature take its course.

"That most of the evidence relied on by the prosecution was entirely circumstantial evidence, and not weighty enough to justify conviction. On the contrary, the only direct evidence established the prisoner's innocence.

"That the medical evidence adduced by the prosecution proved that the death might have resulted from natural causes, and that if any operation had been performed it was more likely to have been performed subsequent to Thursday, the 21st July, and when the prisoner was 200 miles away from the deceased, and there was no evidence that he counselled or procured the operation.

"That it is the universal opinion that the verdict was not justified by the evidence, and we, therefore, humbly submit that the prisoner should have been acquitted.

"That the prisoner enlisted as a gunner in the Royal Artillery in October, 1869, was promoted to a bombardier in January, 1872, made a corporal in 1872, sergeant in 1874, battery sergeant-major in 1878, warrant-officer in November, 1883, and got his commission as lieutenant in 1889. He served in India for a period of fourteen years, from 1875 to 1889. He was through the Afghan War, was at Kandahar, and wears the medal for the Afghan War. On obtaining his commission he was within a few months made Adjutant of the 2nd Volunteer Artillery in Liverpool. He remained in Liverpool for five years and ten months, and then rejoined his regiment. The prisoner during his many years' service in the ranks bore an irreproachable character both as a soldier and as a man, and after being commissioned he was respected by his brother officers and men of all ranks. His moral character was never questioned until the unfortunate infatuation which has brought about his present position became known. He has four sons now serving in her Majesty's Army. His wife and four young children are left totally unprovided for.

"That your memorialists humbly submit that the terrible ordeal through which the prisoner has passed, the forfeiture of his position, and the loss of his pension after thirty years' service are more than sufficient punishment for any moral crime he may have committed.

"Your memorialists therefore humbly pray that you will recommend the case of this prisoner to the favourable consideration of the Crown, and advise her Majesty to exercise her gracious pardon.

"And your memorialists will ever pray, etc."

The petition was made in vain, and Lieutenant Wark is now undergoing his sentence of three years' penal servitude practically for, being a married man, having written indecent or voluptuous letters to a woman he had loved not wisely but too well.

APPENDIX.

THE CASE OF LIEUTENANT WARK.

THE MEDICAL EVIDENCE.

DR. FRANK THOMAS PAUL was examined by Mr. Pickford. He said:—I am a fellow of the Royal Society, honorary surgeon to the Liverpool Royal Infirmary, and professor of medical jurisprudence in the Victoria University. On the date after the death of Miss Yates I, in the presence of Drs. Brigg, Bligh, and Shaw, made a post-mortem examination of her body. We found that the cause of death was simply septic peritonitis and pleuritis—blood-poisoning.

Was there any indication of any illness, except that, which would cause death?

None. The body generally was healthy with these exceptions. I found upon opening the abdomen that there was peritonitis, and that the cause of that was inflammation of a similar kind in the womb. The womb was considerably enlarged. There was a small abrasion in the neck of the womb. The chest, heart, and lungs were healthy, but there was some thin matter in the pleural cavity. The deceased was pregnant, and there was abortion, which was shown by the size and character of the womb. The abortion set up septic inflammation which caused death. There was no more congestion of the lungs than one would find resulting from blood-poisoning.

With regard to the abrasion, can you speak positively as to how it was caused?

I cannot. It was a very slight abrasion. It might have been caused by the use of any instrument in the womb.

Have you seen that catheter?—(instrument produced).

I have.

Is that an instrument which might cause the abrasion?

I think it might do.

From appearances alone can you say positively whether it was a natural miscarriage, or one produced by instruments?

Witness: *There was nothing in the appearance of the parts which would justify me in stating whether it was a natural miscarriage, or one produced by instruments. In many cases of the kind it is impossible to say whether an instrument has been used or not. Where the womb is not injured you cannot tell,* but in other cases it is possible to speak positively. This is a case in which I could not speak positively.

MR. PICKFORD: You have heard the evidence in this case?

I have.

(37)

MR. GILL: I object to an expert witness being asked to express an opinion upon other evidence.

MR. PICKFORD: The question is this—Assuming the instrument to have been used six or seven days before for the purpose of procuring abortion, are the appearances consistent with the use of such an instrument?

WITNESS: They are, my lord.

THE JUDGE: That is, successfully used?

Yes, my lord.

In reply to further questions from MR. PICKFORD, the WITNESS said he saw the fœtus, but could not say how long it was dead.

HIS LORDSHIP: Or how old it was?

About four months.

Cross-examined by MR. GILL: You have said before, I believe, that the abrasion in the womb might have been caused by the use of the curette?

WITNESS: Yes.

Now, what was there in the post-mortem appearances, apart from that slight abrasion, to suggest that this was not a natural miscarriage?

WITNESS: There was nothing else suggested by the post-mortem.

There are a considerable number of miscarriages from natural causes?

WITNESS: There are.

And the third or fourth month is, perhaps, the commonest time for miscarriages to take place?

About the third month.

There are a variety of causes which predispose to miscarriage?

Oh, yes.

And there are cases in which women produce miscarriage themselves?

There are, no doubt, cases in which they produce miscarriage themselves.

Have you read of cases in which women have procured miscarriage by the use of knitting-needles, pieces of wire, whalebone, stilettoes or hair-pins, bugies or catheters?

WITNESS: I have heard of them.

MR. GILL: This catheter is called a soft, gum-elastic catheter?

Yes.

And it is used for drawing off water?

That is its proper purpose.

Upon opening the uterus did you find a large piece of the placenta retained?

I did.

In ordinary miscarriages the question of getting away the placenta is a matter of the greatest importance?

It is.

HIS LORDSHIP: It does not necessarily go away of itself?

Not necessarily.

If any part of the placenta is retained it is highly dangerous to the patient?

Yes, it is highly dangerous, because it may putrify and so set up blood-poisoning.

And in this case the examination showed that blood-poisoning had existed there?

Yes, blood-poisoning had existed, certainly.

And the way to get the whole of the after-birth away would be by curetting?

Yes, I believe that is the practice of specialists in that department.

Having scraped the walls of the uterus with that instrument, and removing any remaining portion of the placenta the next thing would be to use the uterine douch with an anti-septic?

WITNESS: That is the common practice.

In this case you said that the abrasion might very well be caused by the curette?

Yes.

What is about the proportion of natural miscarriages—would you put it at one in five or more?

WITNESS: I should have thought it was rather less than that, but I would rather not answer that question. There is authority for saying that there are miscarriages from one out of five to one out of ten pregnancies. I don't mean this sort of miscarriage, but ones that take place earlier.

MR. GILL: The question as to whether a person is likely to miscarry greatly depends upon the state of her health?

WITNESS: Yes, undoubtedly.

In reply to further questions DR. PAUL said that the left kidney in deceased was normal, but the right was enlarged. That condition had no bearing upon her death.

What are the conditions likely to give rise to a natural miscarriage?

WITNESS: Well, there is a constitutional tendency in a great many people, and a person having one miscarriage there is a great tendency to have them again. Over-exertion, jolting of any kind, anything that upsets the ovaries or uterine organs.

Would the excitement of excessive sexual intercourse give rise to miscarriage?

HIS LORDSHIP: After three or four months?

WITNESS: It is quite possible, although getting perhaps less likely. Up to three or four months it would be quite likely to do it.

MR. GILL: It is one of the reasons given by authorities?

It is unquestionably, especially if the intercourse takes place about the time of the periods.

Is there any other condition of the body which would give rise to it?

WITNESS: Any serious illness would. Anything which would give rise to an inflammatory condition would pre-dispose to abortion.

Fright, of course, is not an uncommon cause?

No; fright is a cause.

Can you tell, at all, with regard to the condition of the lungs how long she had been suffering from the congestion?

I should say it was recent—probably within the last 48 hours.

MR. GILL: Any displacement of the womb has a tendency to produce miscarriage?

Yes.

Sometimes where there is miscarriage, and it is looked after well, you find that slight peritonitis follows, but it passes away and the patient recovers?

WITNESS: Yes, but it is not septic peritonitis.

Is there the slightest difference in the world between peritonitis in a natural miscarriage and peritonitis in an artificially-produced miscarriage unless where matter is introduced into the womb by a poisoned instrument or anything of that sort?

No, the peritonitis would be the same. If septic peritonitis followed it would be fatal.

Septic peritonitis would occur in a woman against whom nothing had been suggested?

Oh, yes.

When that kind of peritonitis—not of a septic character—occurs, does the matter which forms as a result give rise to adhesions, and fix on the uterus?

WITNESS: You have had inflammation of a septic character which does not produce adhesions.

In matter it becomes harder?

It never becomes matter, but only inflammatory exhudations.

THE JUDGE: There the patient would not die?

WITNESS: No.

MR. GILL: It gives rise to adhesions and sometimes fixes on the uterus?

It does.

With regard to the use of the catheter for drawing off water, can a woman easily use it herself?

Oh, yes, when it is explained to her, I should think she ought to be able to do it with ease.

MR. GILL: The time within which miscarriage follows anything done to the womb varies considerably?

Oh, yes.

MR. GILL: Twenty-four hours, two days, and sometimes three days?

WITNESS: Never less than twenty-four hours unless it was produced by a medical man. A very small fœtus may be discharged quickly.

MR. GILL: Supposing the catheter was inserted in a woman with the intention of giving rise to miscarriage, it would be important that the catheter should be retained in its place?

WITNESS: Yes, or roughly used.

MR. GILL: It would be a very difficult thing for a woman to retain the catheter unless she was lying down?

I believe it will stop in when the woman is walking about. I have no personal experience, but I understand it will.

Did you see the prescription that was found in the woman's room—of Epsom salts and hot gin?

I did.

Would the taking of medicines of a weakening character be likely to give rise to miscarriage?

It would encourage a tendency to it.

If the tendency was there?

Abortive medicines are more often violent purgatives than anything else.

THE JUDGE: Would it do that after three or four months?

WITNESS: Not unless the person was predisposed to it.

MR. GILL: The ordinary way to procure abortion would be by passing a syringe into the uterus?

WITNESS: A specialist would not do it that way. When we do it we do it by dilating the uterus, and taking it away in a more scientific manner.

Did you see the fœtus at all?

I only saw it after it was preserved for some time.

Do you think it would be easy to express an opinion as to the length of time a fœtus had been dead by looking at it?

I think an expert in that department would be able to give a very good opinion of it.

THE JUDGE: It was said that he could not give as good an opinion as if he had seen it fresh.

MR. GILL: Wouldn't it be an exceedingly difficult thing to express an opinion as to the length of time it was dead *in utero* to a few days?

Yes, to a few days. The changes are slow.

MR. GILL: The common cause of abortion is the death of the fœtus in the uterus for some reason or other?

I should think that is the commonest cause, that is, at the early stages of pregnancy. I would not like to say that it was so in the later stages.

You say you have seen cases of that kind, where the fœtus has died in the uterus?

I see a great many every year.

Tell me some of the causes?

It is generally something which interferes with the nutrition.

MR. GILL: What other kind of disease in the mother would give rise to the death of the fœtus *in utero*?

Syphilis is certainly one cause.

Is that a common cause?

Amongst the lower classes it is a fairly common cause.

And in those cases where the expulsion of the fœtus takes place after its death very often the placenta is retained?

WITNESS: I don't think I should speak from experience. My experience is from examining specimens.

Apart from what you noticed in this particular case, is kidney disease a cause of miscarriage—is it one of the common causes given in the text-books as explaining how abortion arises?

I should think only when the kidney disease is advanced; but I don't call this really kidney disease. I think her kidneys were doing their duty. I mean that they were performing the functions that kidneys are asked to perform.

What was it that gave rise to one of the kidneys being double the size of the other?

It was simply dilation of the pelvis. The probability is that she had some illness that produced it, and escaped afterwards, some accidental cause perhaps which gave rise to dilation first of all.

What would be the size of this kidney which was diseased—what would it hold? Would it hold a pint?

WITNESS: I should not have thought more than half a pint. It is no uncommon thing for them to hold a great many pints; they hold a gallon sometimes.

When was the catheter first shown to you?

I don't know the date. I believe it was shortly after the death of the woman.

Supposing that catheter had blood upon it, how long would you expect the blood to remain without drying?

Unless it was in a moist place it would dry in a few hours. If it were in the sun it would quickly dry; but if it were clotted in the mouth of the catheter it would not dry for a few hours.

Re-examined by MR. PICKFORD: Supposing the abrasion on the uterus had been caused by the catheter, could you judge from the position of that abrasion that it was done by the woman herself?

WITNESS: I thought most likely due to the wearing of the catheter on that spot.

Do you think it was inserted by herself?

I don't think it is likely that she would insert the catheter herself into the womb.

THE JUDGE: Can you tell us why?

WITNESS: It is a difficult thing to do. A doctor takes some time over it. It has often been pushed right through the womb.

MR. PICKFORD: You were asked about inflammation in septic cases which might produce adhesions, causing peritonitis—would you find signs of it in the post-mortem examination?

WITNESS: Oh, yes.

Did you find any in this case?

No.

You were asked about the proportion of miscarriages to conceptions—is that very much smaller as they get towards four months?

Yes.

Is a natural miscarriage at the age of four months a common or an uncommon occurrence?

It is an uncommon thing, I should think.

THE JUDGE: There was a large piece of placenta adhering to the uterus. I want to know do you mean that the poisoning that was found was due to the retention of the placenta?

WITNESS: It might have been due to the abortion if it had been produced by the catheter. The catheter is a dangerous instrument to use. It might take in along with it germs from the vaginal passage, and if allowed to remain there these would produce inflammation.

MR. GILL: Ignoring the abrasion for a moment, was not what you saw there of the retained placenta abundant evidence as to its being the origin of the peritonitis?

WITNESS: It is probably the usual cause of blood-poisoning afterwards. That would be sufficient cause.

THE JUDGE: You told Mr. Gill that a catheter, for the purpose of procuring abortion, must be roughly used so as to break up the fœtus, or should be retained in its place for some time—what time?

WITNESS: A day, I should say.

How would it operate then?

WITNESS: You gradually set up contraction of the uterus, and it begins to expel the catheter as a foreign body and so expel the fœtus with the catheter.

A JUROR here remarked: I understand from this gentleman that he said that when he made an examination of the body there was nothing to show that it might not be an ordinary miscarriage. We want to understand that.

THE JUDGE, by way of answer, read his notes of DR. PAUL'S evidence.

DR. HENRY BRIGGS, examined by MR. PICKFORD, related how he visited the patient at 140 Salisbury Road three times. He saw the fœtus there, and he judged it was four months old. It was not dead in the womb more than two or three days, at the very outside. He attended the post-mortem, and he entirely agreed with the evidence given by Dr. Paul.

Do you also agree with him that in the post-mortem appearances themselves there was nothing to enable anyone to say with certainty whether it was a natural miscarriage or one that was artificially produced?

WITNESS: The appearances were consistent with natural miscarriage.

Assuming that the miscarriage had been produced by the use of an instrument like a catheter a few days before, were the appearances consistent with that?

Yes, but they do not enable me to say positively.

Are they consistent with the use of the catheter on the 20th or 21st?

WITNESS: Oh, quite.

Do you also agree with Dr. Paul that the abrasion was consistent with the use of the catheter or curette?

Yes, either one or the other.

What do you say as to the probability of her being able to do it herself?

WITNESS: I think it would be difficult for a patient to do it for herself.

You are a specialist in diseases of women, and have many cases coming under your notice, have you any knowledge of a woman having used a catheter herself?

No.

Have you found a record in the books?

I have found one; but one finds instances of knitting-needles, pieces of wire, and such like. The catheter is more difficult.

Is it harder or easier for a woman to use a catheter?

It is harder. The object of the catheter is that it should do no damage, if skilfully used.

You saw Miss Margaret Yates after her sister's death?

I did.

Was she in a mental condition to give evidence?

She was not, I advised her to be sent away.

MR. PICKFORD: I should like to know this—Supposing a month or two before this, there had been one or two attempts, and that they failed, would that make it easier for the catheter to be inserted?

Oh, easier, supposing the catheter entered the womb.

The more suppuration and irritation the more abortion would be produced?
Yes.

Assuming it to be the case that such attempts had been made at the beginning of June or the beginning of July, would it be necessary to leave the catheter in, or would it be necessary to use force?

I think less force would be necessary, but the previous use of the catheter would have opened the canal a little more.

Answering a question by the JUDGE, DR. BRIGGS said that if attempts had been twice made by a stranger it would be easier for the woman herself to insert the catheter afterwards.

Cross-examined by MR. GILL: We have heard of abortions being produced by passing a catheter into the neck of the uterus?

WITNESS: I say it must go beyond the neck as a rule. It would not produce suppuration in the fœtal gathering if it did not.

How long is it necessary to leave a foreign body like a catheter in the body to produce miscarriage?

That varies in different individuals. In some women abortion follows very slowly, and it may not come off at all. The average time is from twenty-four to thirty-six hours. The time may be shorter but it seldom occurs. I never use a catheter myself. I use a boogia, an instrument like a syphon.

You have had large experience in dealing with women?

Yes.

As a result of the post-mortem examination in this case what was there presented to you to show that this was not an ordinary miscarriage?

WITNESS: Nothing, unless the abrasions.

Do you agree also that the abrasion was one that could be perfectly well caused by the curette?

WITNESS: Quite.

However carefully a curette is used I suppose a slight abrasion may occur?

Yes.

What do you say are the causes that give rise to natural miscarriage?

WITNESS: The constitutional state of the parents, such as kidney disease, syphilis, lead poisoning, or any constitutional state of debility; and the local causes are numerous.

Is it not frequently a cause of miscarriage that the fœtus dies in the womb and is expelled by itself?

Yes.

Isn't it quite possible for a woman to use the catheter upon herself?

It is possible, but it would be very difficult.

Haven't you yourself described it as quite possible but not very easy?

Yes.

And at the time that you were giving your evidence you were under the impression that you had read of some instances of women using catheters themselves?

Yes, and I read up and could not find them.

When you saw the deceased woman on the Tuesday did you do anything to her?

I saw that it was absolutely useless.

THURSDAY, DECEMBER 8TH.

Evidence for the prosecution, continued:—

DR. JOHN BLIGH, examined by MR. TOBIN, said that he was physician to the Yates family for a number of years. On the day before Jane Yates's death, he heard of her serious illness at 140 Salisbury Road, and he went there alone the first visit, but subsequently for consultation with Drs. Briggs and Shaw. He was shown the fœtus by Dr. Shaw, and he agreed that it was about four months old. He formed the opinion that it was dead about a week—any time between three and six days. On the morning of her death, after exchanging views with the two other doctors, he went upstairs and saw Miss Yates. He put some questions to her which she answered, and he embodied her answers in a statement which he read over to her. He then handed the paper to her and she signed it. She answered somewhat hesitatingly, and she knew she was dying.

MR. TOBIN here handed in the document, which was in the following terms:—"I make this statement in the presence of Nurse Rendall and my sister, Miss M. Yates, that I produced the miscarriage myself, from the effects of which I am now suffering, and that I accuse no person of instrumental interference in its production, and that I have been strongly advised to the contrary.—Signed Jane Yates, 27th July."

WITNESS continued: On the next day I went to Mrs. Yates's house in Edge Lane. I don't know whether a police officer was with me or not—I believe he was not, the first time. In the bedroom which had been occupied by the deceased I saw the brown bag which had been brought from 140 Salisbury Road. On opening the bag I found a catheter in it, wrapped in cotton wool, and there was a handkerchief or towel around the cotton wool.

Was there any blood?

Yes, a considerable amount of blood on the top of the instrument.

Was the blood wet or dry?

It was semi-fluid.

Was there blood on the cotton wool?

Yes, a portion of the cotton wool lay in front of the eye of the catheter. It was partially coagulated in the interstices.

Supposing the instrument had been in that sanitary towel for some little time, can you form any idea of how long it was there?

It would be about seven days there—for this reason, that it was hermetically sealed. I mean that the air could not get into the catheter. I was present at the post-mortem examination, and I quite agree with what Dr. Paul has said.

Cross-examined by MR. GILL: Had you recently attended the deceased girl before her death?

Yes, I saw her on the 3rd, 6th, and 9th of May.

What was the matter with her then?

Bronchial catarrh.

At that time did you visit her at her house?

Yes, once.

Had you seen her in July at all?

I don't think so.

Have you any distinct recollection as to whether you have seen her in July?

Professionally, I have not.

THE JUDGE: But you may have seen her?

I don't think so; I was attending her mother who was ill.

Did you know of her suffering from congestion of the lungs?

No.

Had you prescribed for her recently?

On the 6th of May.

Do you keep a record of your prescriptions?

Yes, most of them.

I understand that when you saw Dr. Shaw in the first instance you were invited to go to the house, and did you refuse?

Yes.

And then, I understand, you went into the house alone and saw her?

I drove to her mother's house in Edge Lane. She had just gone on to see her daughter, and I followed her to Salisbury Road.

Did you see the deceased alone?

I did.

Did you know that she had been curetted the day before?

I only saw her as a friend; I didn't interfere with her treatment at all.

When you came there later in the day was it after Dr. Briggs had seen her?

Yes, I understood that Dr. Briggs wished to see me there. I saw him after he had examined the deceased.

Were you present when the examination was made by Dr. Briggs in the presence of Dr. Shaw?

I was.

Did you know then that she had been curetted the day before?

Yes, Dr. Shaw said so.

I understand that your position was that you were not advising at all?

Yes. I went there in the interest of the mother.

Have you had experience yourself in the treatment of natural miscarriages?

Yes.

And have you had experience of cases of peritonitis in natural miscarriages?

Yes.

Does peritonitis in cases of natural miscarriages arise from part of the placenta being retained?

Sometimes.

And the curette is used for the purpose of removing the remainder of the placenta?

It is.

If there is reason to suppose that any part of the placenta is remaining in the uterus an instrument of that kind is used for detaching or removing it?

It may or it may not.

Would it be the right thing to do?

Decidedly, that is the practice.

MR. GILL: If one is competent to do it—do you use the curette?

Yes, when it is necessary.

And using it the object would be to pass the curette through the neck of the uterus, and then to scrape the wall of the uterus to get away the remains of the *débris* there?

Yes.

Then the answer is hardly correct that it may or may not be used?

WITNESS: It may be removed by the finger. Wherever there is a doubt of a portion of the after-birth being retained it is a duty to remove it with the finger, before the parts become shrunken.

MR. GILL: If a woman has natural miscarriage, and she is fortunate enough to have medical assistance immediately after the miscarriage takes place, the attention of the medical man would be directed to removing the placenta?

Quite so.

And then he would endeavour to remove it with the finger?

Yes.

And after some time has passed isn't the curette used?

Yes.

And having removed it you would then by the uterine douch clean out the uterus?

Yes; it sometimes sloughs away of itself.

And while there is any there there is danger?

Yes.

When you saw the dying woman on the Wednesday morning did you see her for the purpose of taking from her a dying statement?

I did not see her for that purpose.

Was it on the suggestion of Dr. Shaw, or Dr. Briggs, or both, that you were selected to take from her a dying statement?

Yes, Dr. Briggs suggested it. After the consultation downstairs with the doctors, at the request of one I went up a second time to take her dying statement.

As deceased was considered to be *in extremis* it was deemed advisable to ask her to make a statement?

Yes.

And you volunteered to ask her?

Yes.

Did you ask her positively if anyone had used an instrument upon her?

I did, and she answered me very hesitatingly.

What did you ask her? Is this what you said on a previous occasion? "I asked her positively if anyone had used an instrument upon her. She denied it, and she said she was to blame herself"—is that the correct description?

Yes.

I dare say you recognise that this is your own description of what took place?

Practically.

MR. GILL: "I again pressed her to make a statement and she made one to me"—is that correct?

WITNESS: Yes—hesitatingly.

Did you in your evidence before the magistrate or before the coroner say that she made her statement hesitatingly?

I don't think I did, I was not asked.

Did she ask you if she was going to die?

Yes.

Did you tell her that she would not live?

I did.

Did you again press her to make a statement?

I did.

And was it after that she made the statement which you subsequently wrote out?

Did you write out what you believe was the substance of her statement?

I did.

THE JUDGE: She didn't dictate it to you word for word as you wrote it out?

No.

Mr. Gill: Nor did you reproduce, of course, question and answer?

I did not.

Were you in any way being hurried by the other doctors?

They were waiting downstairs for me, and I was told that Dr. Briggs was in a hurry to go. That was as I was concluding the statement that she made.

Mr. Gill: That is to say, the writing of it out after you had ceased to question her?

Is this your description with regard to it?—"The doctors were downstairs. In consequence of their hurry I could not make the statement so full and complete as I wished, but the substance of deceased's replies are embodied in it. It was my interpretation of what she said to me, and she signed this statement after I had handed it to her to read."

Witness: Yes; that is my description of it; I did say that.

Were the questions you asked in a voice sufficiently loud to be heard by the nurse, do you know?

I don't think so; the nurse was near the window.

Did the nurse leave the room during the time you were asking the questions?

She may have.

You afterwards went downstairs and showed the statement to the two doctors?

Yes.

When you saw the fœtus did you form any impression that it was a three months' fœtus?

I said that I thought it was three or four months. I said it after a casual glance at it.

Was this your first account of this matter—"On Tuesday Dr. Shaw showed me a fœtus about three months developed"?

Yes, I said that casually.

Do you mean that when you were giving your evidence in the case you gave your evidence casually?

I do not.

I suggest to you that when you gave your evidence before the coroner that was what you said—that it was a three months' fœtus?

Yes, I think I said so.

Did you subsequently say that it was about four months?

About three or four months; that was what I meant.

Would it be difficult to form an opinion, looking at the fœtus in a casual way, how long it had been dead?

Generally, from the colour of it, and a casual glance, you can form an estimate.

In a casual glance would it be difficult to form an opinion as to how long it had been dead?

To the exact time it would.

Would you undertake to say, from the casual observation that you speak of, that that fœtus had been dead more than two days?

I would assume that it was dead three or four days.

Or two or three days at the outside?

It might be longer. It depends on the health of the fœtus altogether. I looked at it without touching it. I did not make a medical examination by instruments.

The same casual examination from which you formed the opinion that it was about three months developed?

About three months.

Have you had cases of natural miscarriage from the fœtus dying in the womb?

I have.

From some disease, perhaps, that the mother was suffering from?

From some cause—generally from a fall, a shock, or lifting heavy weights.

Or from constitutional reasons?

Yes, sometimes.

When you went to the house with the mother, and got into the room, did you examine, in any way, the contents of the room?

I did.

THE JUDGE: That is, the deceased girl's room?

Yes.

MR. GILL: Did you see marks of blood in the room?

Yes.

Vaginal syringes?

I saw a case which contained one.

And things for cutting corns?

I don't think I noticed that.

You remember giving your account of the finding of that catheter?

Yes.

Was this the account you gave of it—"After the death I went into the deceased's bedroom, in Edge Lane, and on going over some things there, and on searching the brown bag, with the deceased's mother, a small square box was found, and in it a catheter with some cotton wool which was clotted and adhering to it"?

That is correct.

The catheter was found at the bottom of the box?

WITNESS: What I understood by the box is that it was not in the box that contained the fœtus.

Was any catheter found in the box where the fœtus was?

No.

Was there anyone else there besides you when the room was searched?

The mother, and I think there was a police officer.

How many times did you search the room?

I think I was three times in the room.

Was it for the purpose of searching the room or merely to look at it?

I went there on purpose to see what she had to show:

What interval was there between your visits?

I think about a day or so.

Assuming that a soft gum-elastic catheter can be inserted into the uterus, within what time would you expect uterine action to be set up that might expel the fœtus?

WITNESS: It might occur at any time from six hours to two or three days.

A gum-elastic catheter subject to heat becomes very soft?

Yes.

It would alter its course more easy than a solid, rigid thing?

Yes.

If you pass a catheter with a stilette into the body it will go straight, but a soft gum-elastic catheter without anything in it, wouldn't it yield to the slightest resistance?

Yes, it would alter its course.

Wouldn't it, with the warmth of the body, double?

Not exactly double.

Handling the catheter will make it pliable?

Yes.

And passing a catheter into the body of a woman you intend to pass it so as to get into the neck of the uterus at once?

There would be a difficulty.

It would be some time before the neck of the uterus was found?

Yes.

Have you ever known of a case of a soft gum-elastic catheter without any stilette having passed into the uterus?

Never.

THE JUDGE: You have never known a catheter employed?

MR. GILL: That was not my question.

WITNESS: Personally, I have never known it.

MR. GILL: In your opinion could a soft gum-elastic catheter be passed into the uterus?

With assistance it could.

THE JUDGE: With assistance, not by the person herself?

No, my lord.

MR. GILL: You don't agree with the opinion of Dr. Briggs that it would be quite possible but not very easy?

WITNESS: In some instances, yes; but, generally speaking, I think it next to an impossibility.

Then you don't agree with him?

Not exactly.

Had you during the last three or four years been treating the deceased to any course of medicine?

Yes.

For what?

I treated her once for sore throat, about three years ago—two or three years ago.

What did you treat her for?

I think it was anti-syphilitic treatment. The throat was sore.

THE JUDGE: Was it a kind of sore throat which might be due to syphilis?

Yes, my lord, but I did not mention it to her.

What would be the course of treatment—mercurial treatment?

Yes.

How often did you treat her for that?

I saw her but once; I understood her to be under the treatment of another medical man.

Re-examined by MR. PICKFORD: How long were you treating her for sore throat?

I saw her but once.

Were you treating her for anything else?

For a cold only.

THE JUDGE: Had she any in the nature of syphilis then?

No, my lord.

What time was that?

It was some time in May, or perhaps before that month. I was to see her mother, and I treated the daughter for cold. I told her what to do.

MR. PICKFORD: Did you know she had been absent from home?

WITNESS: I knew she had been away on a journey.

You treated her in March and May of the year in which she died?

Yes.

Without one exception had you treated her at all except for sore throat?

No.

When you treated her in March was there any trace of syphilis then?

WITNESS: No trace whatever.

From what you saw two or three years ago of her condition, when you suspected syphilis, was there anything in her condition then which you would think would produce liability to miscarriage?

WITNESS: If I apprehend you aright, I don't think so.

Do you think there was anything constitutional that would render her liable to miscarriage?

Oh, no. People are treated for syphilis when they are in the family way, and it saves the child and the mother.

My friend has asked you what might be done with a soft catheter—when cold is it soft?

No.

Do you think that the time required to pass it through the neck of the uterus would soften it?

It would slightly soften it.

Would a minute be long enough to materially soften it?

No.

Supposing it were passed into the uterus you think it would set up uterine action even if soft?

Yes, certainly; it is for that object.

Do you know what kind of curette was used by Dr. Shaw?

I don't know.

THE JUDGE: Did you professionally examine her during her last illness?

Yes.

Did she seem to be suffering from cold, or congestion of the lungs?

She seemed to be in pain in different parts of the body and chest. The pulse was uncountable; she was breathing with difficulty.

What did you trace that to?

I understood it to be septic inflammation due to blood-poisoning, and not due to an independent attack of congestion in the chest.

———

DR. HUGH T. SHAW, examined by MR. PICKFORD, said he was M.D. and Master in Surgery, practising in Liverpool. He had known the deceased,

Miss Yates, for several years, and had attended her professionally before this pregnancy.

When did you begin to attend her professionally?

In 1895.

What did you attend her for then?

Sore throat.

That would be about the same time that Dr. Bligh spoke of?

I think it would be, but I am not sure.

What was the sore throat due to?

Syphilitic virus.

How long was she under treatment for that?

A few weeks.

Can you tell me whether she was then at home, or staying away?

She was staying away at the time.

Was she then better?

The throat improved.

Was she well when you ceased to treat her?

I don't think so.

When did you see her again professionally?

About ten months before her death.

That would bring us to September, 1897?

Yes.

What did you treat her for then?

Neuralgia.

Did you examine her then at all for syphilitic affection?

No, but I thought the neuralgia might be due to the same cause.

How long was she under your treatment then?

I gave her a prescription, and I did not see her afterwards. I told her how to use the ointment to relieve the pain, and I didn't see her again.

When did you see her next?

I didn't see her until the end of June.

What did she come to consult you about at the end of June?

About the cessation of the menstrual flow.

And did you examine her?

I did.

Was she pregnant?

She was.

About how long had she gone pregnant?

I judged from examination about two or three months.

MR. PICKFORD said he had a question to ask the witness as to the conversation which he had at that interview with the deceased woman, but he would first take the opinion of the Court as to whether he was legally entitled to put it.

MR. GILL: The question was not admissible. He objected to it, on the ground that a conversation in June upon an indictment which charged the commission of an act of murder on the 20th of July was not relavant. The view of his friend for the prosecution was the correct view.

MR. PICKFORD: I don't express any view.

MR. GILL: I don't attach any importance to it, but I don't want to appear to accept evidence which I think is not admissible apart from its importance.

THE JUDGE asked MR. PICKFORD what his question was?

MR. PICKFORD: My question is simply this—Did she ask for any remedy for her condition? Perhaps that is open to objection as a leading question.

THE JUDGE: Oh, no, not to a medical man.

MR. GILL: Well, I saw it is not evidence. I don't desire to appear to object to it, because it might place me in a position with the jury of thinking that I desire to shut out something important.

THE JUDGE: I have thought this matter over, and I think it of importance chiefly because I think that it would, possibly not be in this case, but in many cases, extremely injurious to the ends of justice if such questions as this were not admitted. I think we should have the full evidence before the tribunal. In this case there is evidence fit to be laid before a jury of a common purpose between the deceased woman and the man who is a prisoner in the dock. I don't say that the jury are bound to find a common purpose. If they find there is no common purpose then they must omit all the acts of Jane Yates. Many acts given in evidence would be inadmissible against the prisoner, but if there is a common purpose or, in the view of the jury, a common purpose between Jane Yates and the prisoner, every act done by Jane Yates is evidence against the prisoner just as if Jane Yates were alive and she was being tried for felony or procuring her own miscarriage. Every act of hers would be evidence against her. Very often an act of pantomime or a sign would be evidence, but speech is a more effective way of describing what might be done. Statements of past events are not evidence. I shall not allow any question to be asked of Dr. Shaw as to any statement with reference to a previous act of conduct of the prisoner, but I shall allow anything in the nature of a request made by Jane Yates, or counsel asked for by Jane Yates, which can be considered in furtherance of a common object. Do you understand me?

MR. PICKFORD: Yes, my lord.

DR. SHAW, who had for the moment retired from the witness-box, was then recalled.

MR. PICKFORD: On this occasion did she ask you for any remedy?

WITNESS: She did. She asked me if I could prescribe for her to get her out of her trouble.

And you declined?

Yes.

When did you see her next?

The first or second week in July; it would probably be about the 8th or 9th.

What did she consult you about then?

She did not consult me at all in reference to her condition.

She merely saw you as a friend?

No.

When did you see her again?

She called on the 15th, but I was out; I did not see her.

And when did you see her again?

On the 22nd, the Friday before she died.

What did she consult you about then?

She called, as she expressed it, to see when I was going on my holidays.

Did she make any request to you then?

None whatever.

THE JUDGE: That is, the night of the thunder-storm?

Yes.

What time did she come?

About half past six.

MR. PICKFORD: You have no entry of this visit?

No.

She asked you in the first instance to give her medicine to relieve this condition—had she made any other request to you?

I am not sure whether she made a subsequent request or not, but I don't think so.

You have heard those letters in which "S." is referred to?

Yes.

That "S." refers to yourself?

It does.

MR. PICKFORD: "You cannot, love, expect S. to run any risks for you, but you should expect me to do so"—that refers to you?

Yes.

MR. PICKFORD: In a letter dated July 13th he writes to her—"I would use another thing besides a catheter, and I would ask S. to lend it." Had you been asked to lend it?

DR. SHAW: There was never any request made to me for an instrument. The request was for medicine.

MR. PICKFORD: I understand you don't remember the date exactly, but that it was at the end of June?

WITNESS: The last week in June.

Just think whether any request was made subsequent to the one that you speak of.

Never.

Are you sure?

I am sure.

I think she came to you on the 22nd of July—what did she consult you about?

THE JUDGE: She came to see if he was going on his holidays.

WITNESS: She made no reference to herself at all.

MR. PICKFORD: When did she come to you next?

On July 25th.

How did she describe her symptoms?

She said she was suffering terrific pains in the lower part of the abdomen.

Did you examine her?

Yes, she looked as if she had lost blood.

Did she tell you anything had happened to her?

She did; she said that something had come away from her, and that she had it in a box in the cab outside.

What did you advise her to do?

I advised her to go home.

What then?

She refused to go.

Where did she want to go to?

To the London and North-Western Hotel, Liverpool.

We know she did not go there—why was that?

MR. GILL objected to the question, but the JUDGE allowed it to be answered.

WITNESS: I advised her to go to Mrs. Jackson's. I knew she would get every attention there.

MR. PICKFORD: She did go there, and went to bed?

Yes.

And did you go to see her there?

Yes.

And you examined her?

I did, about half past three o'clock the same day.

What did you find?

I found a number of clots of blood in the vagina.

Was she wearing anything?

She was wearing an ordinary sanitary towel. I removed that and I examined the uterus.

What did you find?

A piece of putrid placenta protruding from the curvex of the uterus.

Did you remove as much as you could with the finger, and afterwards use the curette?

Yes, the curette and then a douch.

What kind of curette did you use?

It was a large spoon flushing curette?

You then flushed the womb, and you left her?

Yes.

Were you sent for in about an hour?

Yes.

And how did you find her then?

She had intense pain. I administered a hypodermic injection of morphia to cure the pain. I called again about ten o'clock. She had got but very little relief.

What did you do then?

I then recommended that her mother and Dr. Bligh should be communicated with.

And did you communicate with them that night?

No, early next morning.

That was at her wish?

Oh, yes, her special wish that I should not communicate until next morning.

You saw her early next morning?

Yes, about half past seven.

How did you find her then?

The symptoms were getting worse.

And did you then go straight to Mrs. Yates's house?

Yes, and with her younger sister to Dr. Bligh's.

You saw her afterwards, with Dr. Bligh and Dr. Briggs, and you heard the account they gave of her—is that correct?

Yes.

THE JUDGE: Do you agree that she died of blood-poisoning?

Yes.

MR. PICKFORD: Had you known the prisoner?

Yes, slightly; I beg pardon, I knew him well.

How did you come to know Miss Yates?

I was a member of the riding-class in connection with the 2nd Lancashire Volunteer Artillery, and I met her there.

Did you receive this letter, and can you tell us the date of it (letter handed to witness), and is it in the prisoner's handwriting?

It is. There is no date to it, but the envelope is marked "July 28th, Woolwich."

SIR HERBERT STEPHEN (clerk) then read the letter:—"Dear Shaw,—How are things shaping? I went to look for you again last night, but was told you had flown. Would like to have seen Mrs. S., but thought she would not like to have seen me. Is there to be an inquest?—Yours faithfully, R. J. Wark."

Cross-examined by MR. GILL: With regard to this matter of treating the deceased two or three years ago—was that about 1895?

Yes.

You understood afterwards that she had seen Dr. Bligh?

Yes.

The condition that you were treating her for, might that be secondary or tertiary syphilis?

Secondary.

That would appear some time after the syphilis had been contracted?

Yes.

THE JUDGE: Would there be a primary or acute stage before in the same patient?

Yes.

MR. GILL: The signs may pass away, and after some time secondary symptoms might appear, and even tertiary symptoms, syphilis being in the constitution all the time?

Yes.

And persons might suffer from syphilis although there is no sign of it for the moment, until something is disclosed, as for instance, a syphilitic throat?

Yes.

I understood you attended her for two or three weeks—at the time that she came to you was she treated to a course of mercury?

She was, she had been treated before, from what I heard from her own relatives, and from prescriptions she showed me, for two or three years.

Mercury treatment is the recognised treatment to get rid of syphilis?

Yes.

When you saw her the last week in June and found her two and a half months pregnant, did you form any opinion then as to whether she was likely to miscarry?

I thought she might probably miscarry.

THE JUDGE: What! In the natural course?

Yes, my lord.

MR. GILL: Constitutional syphilis is a very common cause of miscarriage?

WITNESS: Very common.

Does it arise by the death of the fœtus in the uterus?

Yes, that is one way, or disease of the placenta.

The placenta as you saw it was offensive?

Very offensive.

Apart from syphilis there are many other causes which give rise to natural miscarriage?

Yes.

When you saw the deceased on the night of the thunder-storm was she looking quite well?

Yes. She said she was terrified of the thunder. It was a violent storm.

Assuming that this miscarriage was not a natural miscarriage—assuming that she was right in supposing that she had produced it herself, if the catheter had been inserted on Friday night I suppose the expulsion of the fœtus might take place some time on Saturday night or Sunday?

It might.

If a catheter were inserted by a woman herself it would be far more likely to remain in if she were lying in bed than if she were moving about?

Oh, yes.

On the Monday when you first saw her, and told her to go home to her bed did she say that she would rather kill herself than that her mother should know of her condition?

She did.

From what you could judge of her she was a woman of strong will?

Very strong.

When you spoke to her at the house in Salisbury Road, of going to tell her mother, did she speak strongly and threaten to jump out of bed if you did so?

Yes.

Was that the reason why you did not at once communicate with the mother?

Yes.

Were you in a position to administer an anæsthetic when you examined her that afternoon?

No.

To satisfactorily curette the uterus it would be desirable to give an anæsthetic?

It would.

THE JUDGE: Why didn't you give one?

WITNESS: There was no time. It was desirable to act at once.

MR. GILL: However carefully and delicately you might use the curette you might cause an abrasion?

Yes.

Dr. Paul told us that the use of the curette might cause an abrasion, and you agree with him?

Quite.

Would you, in your opinion, say that the abrasion was one that you might very well have made in using the curette?

It was.

The blood-poisoning that was set up would be amply accounted for by the retained placenta?

Yes.

Especially if it was decayed from disease?

Yes.

A letter was given to you by Miss Jackson which you subsequently handed over to the police?

Yes.

Have you attended Lieutenant Wark medically while he was in Liverpool?

Yes.

During the time that you knew him did you know of his suffering in any way from syphilis?

No.

THE JUDGE: Do you say that she might have secondary syphilis, and lived with the prisoner and not have given it to him?

Yes, my lord.

It is only given in the primary stage?

In the primary stage.

MR. PICKFORD called his lordship's attention to a letter written in pencil by the deceased, but not sent. He wished to know whether that letter was admissible as evidence.

THE JUDGE: I should say not. It contains no statement made by one of the persons in furtherance of the common purpose.

MR. PICKFORD: A statement as to her condition.

THE JUDGE: Having regard to that letter a question should be asked of Dr. Shaw.

MR. GILL: Will your lordship rule on a letter written and not posted, and not brought to the knowledge of the prisoner, is to be brought into the case?

THE JUDGE: At this moment I don't propose to rule upon that letter at all, but I propose to put a certain question to Dr. Shaw.—(to Dr. Shaw)—Do you remember the day of the thunder-storm?

Yes.

Did she ask you any question about a catheter?

No.

Or about any instrument?

No.

Did you advise her to send for Dr. Bligh?

I advised her to send for Dr. Bligh if anything should occur to her, or in the alternative to go away from home to save her mother's house from disgrace.

MR. GILL: This is the conversation, my lord, which I understand you to say would be admissible.

THE JUDGE: I think this is a very improper interference at this moment. (to witness)—What do you mean by saying " if anything occurred "?

I thought she might abort naturally.

And not artificially?

And not artificially.

HIS LORDSHIP here ruled that the pencilled letter referred to was not admissible.

———— :o: ————

LESSING'S

MINNA VON BARNHELM.

Translated, with an Introduction and Notes, by Major-General Patrick Maxwell.

298 pp.; handsomely printed on art paper. Brocade binding; white and gold backs; gilt tops. Suitable for presentation.

PRESS NOTICES.

"Lessing's comedy, 'Minna Von Barnhelm,' holds a unique place in the literary history of Germany. It was published in 1766, and produced on the stage in 1767. Until that period the German drama was, for the most part, abjectly based on foreign models, chiefly French, and was therefore empty of national ideas and national characteristics. It is, in fact, scarcely going too far to say that anything like a real national drama did not exist. After much experience in dramatic writing, Lessing's literary instincts revolted at this state of things, and the comedy which resulted was properly described by a native critic as the first truly German comedy inspired by German motives, and conceived in a really German spirit, which had appeared on the German stage 'since the antecedent decline in that country of popular dramatic spectacle.' 'Minna Von Barnhelm' may therefore be said to have liberated the German stage from its absurd foreign bondage. Its significance in that respect was soon understood, and as a work of national originality it received a national welcome. Germany, in fact, hailed it with delight; and, as Major-General Maxwell informs us, 'it has retained to this day its hold on German readers and the German stage.' But the comedy has a higher value. Many a book has done much to embitter international feeling, but so, on the other hand, has many a piece of wise literature contributed to calm political passion and reconcile or obliterate national and international antagonisms. Lessing's comedy was, in some degree, a work of this kind. It is supposed, indeed, as the translator reminds us, 'to have contributed in no slight measure to the assuagement of the feeling of mutual rancour which, at the close of the Seven Years' War, and for some time after it, prevailed between Prussia and Saxony.' There is no inherent improbability in the view. The story of the comedy in which move and act the chief characters, Major Von Tellheim, an unemployed Prussian officer, and Minna Von Barnhelm, a young Saxon lady of rank, is just of that kind to please and fascinate the two races to which they severally belong. The Prussians and the Saxons must have perceived that their national traits, so strongly and charmingly embodied in the character of the two noble lovers, were a faithful representation, and that consequently their mutual dislikes were wholly unworthy of them, and discreditable to maintain. The case recalls the saying that 'Books not less than bullets may find their billets in saving nations as in killing rogues.' It is pleasing to think that Lessing's comedy possessed saving grace in so eminent a degree. It is not necessary to describe the work; but it is only just to say that it has been, on the whole, admirably translated by Major-General Patrick Maxwell, and that it forms a most interesting piece of reading. It may be added that a version of it was produced at the Haymarket Theatre in London in the year 1786. A good portrait of Lessing is prefixed to the volume, which is a fine specimen of the arts of the printer and binder."—*Glasgow Herald.*

The University Press, Limited, Watford, London.

Luxuriously bound in Brocade.   3s. 6d. net.

PHRYNE.

A Drama in four Acts and a Prologue with an Introduction.

BY

DEMOCRITUS

(Castelvecchio).

The attractive history of Phryne, one of the most celebrated hetairas of ancient Greece, forms the basis of this drama, which was originally published in the Italian language. The social position of the Greek hetaira at the time of Pericles and Alexander the Great cannot be judged or measured by the position of the courtesan in modern times. As the word itself "Hetaira" or "Hetæra" indicates no opprobrium then was attached to the cultured mistresses of kings, statesmen, and philosophers, and the calling of the hetaira was considered, although not free from blame, an honourable one. The wives of Greek citizens attended exclusively to the household duties, and did not take part in any social function, nor were they sufficiently cultured to interest themselves in the highest aspirations of Greek orators, sculptors, and philosophers. Greek writers are unanimous in stating that the hetaira greatly contributed to the artistic education and culture of the nation, and animated and beautified the social gatherings of educated men, not only in Athens and Corinth, but also in other cities of Hellas. On the other hand, we know from the dialogues of Lucian and from the letters of Alciphron that the calling of even the most celebrated of hetairas was mercenary, that many accumulated great wealth, and that many wealthy citizens were ruined through the luxury and prodigality of their mistresses. We know also of the faithful devotion of hetairas to their lovers, of which Timandra and Theodota, the friends of Alcibiades, are an example.

The play is based entirely on the facts known from ancient writers.

Phryne when arriving at the Greek capital was poor, but made the acquaintance of Hyperides, the great orator, whose wealth she absorbed. In due course she became very rich, and her offer to re-erect Thebes, which, no doubt, was based on morbid vanity, was made to the Senate about ten years after her arrival. Phryne's name has come down to posterity through her having been the model of Apelles' great work *Venus Anadyomene* and of Praxiteles' *Cnidian Aphrodite*.

THE UNIVERSITY PRESS, LIMITED,

WATFORD, LONDON.

10s. Net.

CHAPTERS ON HUMAN LOVE.

By GEOFFREY MORTIMER.

"This work, which deals with the more important phases of the great sex question, will be read eagerly by all who agree with the poet that 'the proper study of mankind is man.' Now it is most extraordinary that while every novel read by a young Englishwoman is based on the passion of love, it is considered among the ignorant and the prudish indecent, if not criminal, to discuss, or inquire as to the elements of which that love is composed. This Mr. Mortimer does fearlessly, and with great ability and clearness. Beginning by the exhibition of the passion in animals, he treats of various forms of sex union that have existed and do exist in the world, and of love customs and rites. In the chapters on Hetairism, or prostitution throughout the ages, a large and very important field of inquiry, as well as the morbid perversions of the sexual instinct both in women and men—the two being a growing evil in these latter days—Mr. Mortimer speaks with all necessary directness. The author speculates in an interesting manner on the connection between the bodily passion called love, and spiritual emotion. It seems there is a most profound alliance between the two, as they spring from a common original—the gratification of the senses. Of this an example was the Christian Agapetœ, or 'beloved ones,' the reputed virgins who lived with clerics and yet professed great devoutness and chastity—'the pest of the Agapetœ . . . this strange name of wife without marriage,' as St. Jerome, denouncing the immorality of the early Christian clerics, called it. A final chapter on 'Free Love Theories' completes a very remarkable book which, almost for the first time in England, attempts to give a systematic, though succinct, account of the most powerful of all human emotions—so powerful, indeed, in its manifestations, that men and women have grown afraid to talk about it, although each of them is the product of that physical sexual contact dignified by the name of 'human love.' This volume ought to be found in the library of every student of sociology."—*Reynolds'*.

❋ TABLE OF CONTENTS. ❋

CHAPTER I.

INTRODUCTORY.

Importance of the Subject of Sex-Love—The Mean between Spiritual and Materialistic Views—Neglect of the Formal Study of Sex in England— What is Love?—Physiological, Philosophic, and Poetic Definitions—Mode of Inquiry.

CHAPTER II.

The Passion in Animals.

Nature's Mating-Time—The Beginnings of Love in the Lower Animals—Mollusca and Crustacea—Spiders—Reproduction of Ants and Bees—Fish and Reptiles—The Wooings of Birds—Their Sentiment and Intelligence—Instances of Love in the Mammalia—Amorous War—The Instinct in Dogs, Horses, and Apes—Summary.

CHAPTER III.

Primitive Human Love.

Descent of Man—The Theory of Promiscuity—Westermarck's Criticism of the Hypothesis—Marriage by Capture—Traces of the Custom—Instances of Feigned Rape—Choice of Suitors exercised by Women—Allurements by Clothing and Decoration of the Person.

CHAPTER IV.

The Origin and Growth of Modesty.

Modesty—What it is, and its Purpose—Shame not Natural—Delicacy demanded from Women—Views of Mary Wollstonecraft on Modesty—The Virtue used as a Means of Masculine Control of Women—Immodesty compatible with Chastity—Virginity as a Commodity—Stringency of Rules of Maidenly Chastity—Tokens of Virginity—Religious Defloration—*Jus primœ Noctis*—Unchastity of Peasantry in parts of Scotland—Chastity among Aztec Women—Sacred Virginity—External Indications of Continence—Bewailing Virginity—Magic Virtue in Virgins.

CHAPTER V.

Forms of Sex Union.

Polygamy—Are Men naturally Polygamous?—Plurality of Wives in Various Nations—The Seraglio—Western Polygamy.

CHAPTER VI.

Forms of Sex Union (*continued*).

Polyandry—In India and Ceylon—In Ancient Sparta and Britain—Women under Polyandry—The Marriage of Near Kin—In Animals and in Man—Is Repugnance to such Unions innate or acquired?—Incestuous Love in Literature—Trial Marriage, and the Custom of Bundling—Child Marriage—Among the Inoits—The Shame of India.

CHAPTER VII.

Human Sexual Selection.

Seeming Vagaries of Natural Choice—Spontaneity of Selection—Mantegazza's "Art of Taking a Wife"—Views of Phrenologists and Others—Schopenhauer's Theory—Difficulty of laying down Rules—Love v. Reason—Instinct as a Guide—The Amative and Cold Temperament—Intellectual Attraction—Cobbett's Advice in the Matter—Attempts towards Definite Principles—Difference between the Love Motives of Men and Women—Tolstoi's Opinion.

CHAPTER VIII.

HUMAN SEXUAL SELECTION (continued).

Transmission of Traits—Influence of Marriage for Good and Ill—Galton and Darwin on Heredity—The Perfectionists—Experiments in Stirpiculture—Scientific Control of Procreation—Sir B. W. Richardson's View—Lack of Parental Responsibility—Neglect of the Study of Human Propagation—The Propaganda of Mrs. Victoria W. Martin—*La Viriculture*, by G. de Molinari—" A Plea for the Unborn."

CHAPTER IX.

CELIBACY.

Celibacy a Phenomenon of Civilisation—Ancient Celibate Sects—Its Origin Religious—Sacerdotal Chastity—St. Paul—Vices resulting from Celibacy —Impeachment of the Practice—Pathology of Celibacy—Sex-Love a Necessity—Effect of Continence on Women—Influence upon Men—Social Influence of the Habitude—Classification of Celibates—"The Unloved"— Spurious Chastity—Voluntary Celibacy.

CHAPTER X.

ROMANTIC LOVE AND CHIVALRY.

The Higher Love dependent on the Imagination—Love in Ancient Egypt— The Freedom of the Women of Thebes—Grecian Love and Marriage— Love among the Romans—Romantic Passion of the Northern Nations— Were the Norsemen Chaste?—The Age of Chivalry—Its Influence upon Women—Poetry of Chivalry—Platonic Love.

CHAPTER XI.

LOVE CUSTOMS AND RITES.

Philters—Former Prevalence of the Use of Excitants to the Passion—The Nature of Aphrodisiacs—Scents—Anaphrodisiacs—Some Love-Charms— The Rite of Circumcision—The Practice Amatory—The Custom among the Ancient Jews and Egyptians—Circumcision in Warfare—Performed upon Women—Hygienic and Moral Value of the Practice—Phallicism— Antiquity of the Cult and Survival of Phallic Practices and Symbols— Dionysia—Origin of the Rites and Introduction of the Observance into Greece—The Orgies—Bacchanalian Mysteries in Rome—Survival of Dionysiac Festivals in India and other Countries.

CHAPTER XII.

ADULTERY AND DIVORCE.

Early Divorce—Among the Ancient Jews—Cruel Penalties for Marital Infidelity—In the East—Punishment in Great Britain—Divorce Laws and Reform.

E

CHAPTER XIII.

HETAIRISM.

Need for Educated Inquiry and Candid Statement on the Question—Antiquity of Prostitution and Prevalence to the Present Time—Short Survey—Courtesans in the Grecian and Roman Civilisations—In the Middle Ages—Causes—Does Marriage perpetuate the Evil?—Poverty a Prime Factor—How the Army of Prostitution is Recruited—The Assumption of Necessity—Proposed Remedies—Failure of Suppressive Action—Increase of Venereal Disease—The C.D. Acts—Pathology of the Courtesan—Health of the Class—The Career—Its Stages—The Lower Ranks—The Problem.

CHAPTER XIV.

AMATIVENESS.

Description of the Faculty—Its Potentiality for Good or Ill—Physiological Characteristics of the Amative—Location of "The Organ of Amativeness," by Gall—The Organisation of the Passionate Man and Woman—Facial and other Indications—Normal and Abnormal Amativeness—Erotomania, Satyriasis, and Nymphomania—Testimony of Dr. Maudsley and Dr. Shaw upon Love Neuroses—Shelley and Byron—the Ardent Woman—Influence of Climate on Sexual Passion—Sexuality of Southern and Coloured Races—Restraint upon Sensuality—False Views concerning Amativeness.

CHAPTER XV.

THE PHENOMENON OF FRIGIDITY.

Frequency of Impaired and Absent Sex-Feeling in Modern Women—The Abnormality treated in Fiction—Views of Lácour, and Testimony of Dr. Jordan, Dr. Napheys, Dr. E. J. Tilt, Professor Carl Schroeder, and other Physicians and Doctors—Causes of Sexual Coldness—Moral Impotence—The Defect in Men—Cases Investigated by the Writer—Frigidity not simply a Question for the Pathologist—The Abnormality affects the Character and Views—Mr. D. Christie Murray's criticism of "Jude the Obscure"—A frequent Cause of Conjugal Discord.

CHAPTER XVI.

PERVERSIONS OF THE SEXUAL INSTINCT.

Perversions Common in Primitive and Civilised Nations—Causes—Scientific Opinion on Inverted Sex-Feeling—Masturbation—Sources of the Practice—Ethical and Physiological Views—Evils of the Habit—Its Effect upon the Mind—Homosexuality—Lesbianism—Morbid Sexuality—Necessity for Elimination of Perverted Tendencies through Heredity—Restraint upon the Marriage of Morbid Types and Youthful Environment.

CHAPTER XVII.

CONJUGAL PHYSIOLOGY AND HYGIENE.

The Great Lack of Knowledge of Human Reproduction—Origin of the Ignorance—The Necessity for Inquiry—Sex-Passion in Cultured Races—Hygiene of Marriage—Use and Abuse of Coition—Parentage—Influence of Transitory States on Offspring—Time of Conception—Right Age for Parentage.

CHAPTER XVIII.

THE REAL AND THE IDEAL CONJUGALITY.

Ideal Marriage rarely Realised—The Study of Physiology an Aid in attaining the Ideal—Love Evanescent—Agreement of many of the Highest Minds as to the Law of Change in the Affections—Both Strict Monogamists and Advocates of Dissoluble Unions concur concerning the Mutability of Love —A Common Cause of Unfortunate Conjugality—Disappointment of Women—Why Women are Constant in Marriage—Ideal Union—The Freeing of Women in its Effect on the Sexual Relation—Long Engagements—Reasons for Advocating Short Courtships.

CHAPTER XIX.

INDISSOLUBLE UNIONS.

The Growth and Strengthening of the Monogamic Ideal—Control of the Ancient Church—Early Revolt against Enforced Indissoluble Marriage —Inequalities of Modern Matrimony—Difficulties of Honourable Mutual Separation—The Rise of Discontent with the System of Marriage in England—Godwin, Shelley, and the Owens—Recent Criticisms of Indissoluble Marriage—The Trend of Social Opinion—Dissolution at Will— Rarity of Abiding Affection in Conventional Wedlock—Signs of a New Order—The Future of Love.

CHAPTER XX.

SPIRITUAL LOVE.

Affinity of Mind in Love—Physical Passion Transient—No True Union Without Sex-Magnetism—Asceticism—Debased Views of Physical Love—The Reaction—Elizabeth of Hungary—Theories of Spiritual Love—Culture and the Amative Passion—Sects of Modern Ascetics—"Harmonial Love" —"Karezza," and "Dianism "—"The Kreutzer Sonata "—Æstheticism springs from the Sexual Impulse—"Phases of Love."

CHAPTER XXI.

FREE LOVE THEORIES.

The Ideal of Constancy—Its Rarity—Freedom in Love—The Oneida Experiment—Debate between Horace Greeley, Henry James, and Stephen P. Andrews—"Love v. Marriage "—Views of Emil F. Ruedebusch—The Monogamic Bias—Jealousy—Free Love among the Russian Intelligentia.

The University Press, Limited,

WATFORD, LONDON.

SEAWEED: A Cornish Idyll.

By EDITH ELLIS. (MRS. HAVELOCK ELLIS.)

Price 3s. 6d.

❋ PRESS OPINIONS. ❋

"Deals strenuously, and yet most delicately, with the phase of the old problem which the lives of so many men and women are spent in solving—the mystery of love. Outspoken to a degree, it will inevitably shock prudes. The book will probably find its place on the forbidden list to which the mock modest love to consign the works of George Moore and others, who call a spade a spade, while the same nice-minded censors deal tolerantly enough with the purveyors of filth tied up in rose leaves. But it will delight all who believe in the killing out of the beast in man, and woman too, without the extinction of warm passions."—*Weekly Times and Echo.*

"Edith Ellis revels in absolute liberty; she recognises no fetters whatever, whether imposed by Mrs. Grundy, or the traditions of British fiction."—*Morning Leader.*

"Edith Ellis deserves credit for the simplicity and courage with which she handles a difficult problem."—*Manchester Guardian.*

"Mrs. Ellis has, indeed, been consumed by a passion to penetrate to the subconscious of a woman's nature, to sedulously observe in the development of a woman the working out virtually, despite the will of the woman herself, of forces in her nature which are stronger than that will itself."—*Newcastle Daily Leader.*

"A perfect example of literary art, the like of which we have not seen in England since the days of George Eliot. Kit Trenoweth and his mother are creations in every way as great as Adam and Mrs. Bede. For once in a way that much abused word 'Idyll' has not been profaned; the seven or eight characters who figure in the book stand out as so many clearly-cut cameos which are destined to live in the memory and in literature. The daring psychology of the story is of distinctly educative value, and will be relished by the alert novel reader, who is sickened with the grotesque caricatures, which pass for living pictures, from the brains of so many well-known writers of the present day."—*The Nuneaton Observer.*

"Many readers may object to the boldness of both the plot and its treatment, but there can be no doubt that both are true to nature, and instinct with the real qualities of flesh and blood humanity. 'Seaweed' is indeed an idyll, although a very realistic one. The local colour is strong throughout, and harmonises well with the plain, deep, simple emotions. An occasional humorous interlude enlivens the more pathetic part of this romance of nature, which concludes in the happiest and most-natural manner. 'Seaweed' possesses all the charm of the unconventional, without its frequent faults of exaggeration and eccentricity."—*Saturday Weekly Citizen.*

"To write a story in which the flesh and blood of human nature are shown in their plain reality, while yet infused with an idyllic spirit, is a task much beset with difficulties and dangers. It has, however, been undertaken with a considerable measure of success by Edith Ellis. The interest of the idyll lies as much in the fearless treatment of the plot as with its novelty."—*Glasgow Evening Citizen.*

The University Press, Limited, Watford, London.